THE ESSENTIAL 55

An Award-Winning
Educator's Rules for
Discovering the Successful Student
in Every Child

•

RON CLARK

HYPERION

NEW YORK

Library of Congress Cataloging-in-Publication Data

Clark, Ron
    The essential 55 : an award-winning educator's rules for discovering the successful student in every child / Ron Clark.—1st ed.
      p. cm.
    Includes index.
    ISBN: 1-4013-0001-4
    1. Teaching. 2. Conduct of life. I. Title: Essential fifty-five. II. Title.

LB1025.3 .C534 2003
371.102—dc21

                                        2002032927

FIRST EDITION

10

CONTENTS

ACKNOWLEDGMENTS

Mom and Dad, you are the wisest people I have ever met. Thank you so much for teaching me how to laugh and for showing me how people should be treated. You always supported me and made me feel I could be or do anything that I wanted, and it has, without a doubt, been fun, an adventure, and an honor to be your son.

To my sister, Tassie, thank you for always taking up for me and giving me support. It was nice to know you had my back. Thank you also to Keith for taking care of Tassie and being a great brother-in-law. To Austin, I love you, little buddy. You are one smart boy (always remember, you take after your Uncle Ron), and you have brought a joy and excitement to my life that I had never experienced before. You are destined for greatness.

To Barbara Jones: You are the hardest-working and best teacher I have ever met. I was the luckiest person in the world to have the honor of working by your side. Always remember pretty is as pretty does and "I just got to know what's in that box." Barb, "you my rock."

Thank you to June Zurface, Molly Bowen, Sue Hollowell and all of the exceptional teachers in Aurora who took me in as a skinny, naive boy of 140 pounds and showed me what it means to be a dedicated teacher. Thank you to the community of Aurora for accepting me and supporting all of my unorthodox ideas and projects. I have traveled all over the country this year, and you don't find people any nicer or more genuine than those in Aurora, North Carolina.

Mrs. Rebecca Owens, thank you for being the strictest teacher I ever had. Even when you were fussing at me I could tell you cared. Oh boy was I terrified, but I knew you cared. You taught me a lot, and I miss you. —Bud

Thank you to East Carolina University and the North Carolina Teaching Fellows program for giving me a solid education that was more than books and exams. You molded me into an adult and taught me about compassion, friendship, and how to make a difference. Dr. V, from the moment I first met you, I knew you had your act together, and you never failed to impress me. To Joann Norris and Gladys Graves, you go girls! Work that program!

To the #1 Pirate, Scott Wells, thank you for your belief in this book and for all of your support. Cynthia Adams and Dean Marilyn Sheerer, you are both exceptional ladies, and I love you for all of your energy, help, and kindness.

Mrs. Frances Castillo, when I first got to East Harlem, you took me under your wing, and I stayed there for two years, always under your guidance, support, and love, and I am truly grateful. You are one of the most intelligent, compassionate, and hardworking individuals I have ever met. The work you are doing at PS 83 and in the community of East Harlem is amazing and touches so many lives. I admire and have the utmost respect for you.

Thank you to Vivienne Graham, Brendan Jackson, Hazel Cruz, Liza Ortiz, and all of the other dedicated and driven members of the staff at PS 83 in East Harlem. It was an honor and a pleasure to be part of such an intelligent and hardworking faculty. Thank you Luis for keeping my room spotless, Natalie for feeding me well (I love you), and Alice for making me laugh.

Mary Ellen O'Neill, I admire you so much for your dedication to kids and your determination to make books that are going to make a difference. Working with you has been a joy, and I can't thank you enough for your support of me and this book.

R, Thanks. —R.

Cindy Skaff, it has been an honor and a pleasure to work with you this year. Thank you for helping to schedule all of my speeches and for sharing the same passion for teaching. Everyone at Premiere Speakers Bureau has been amazing, and I am grateful to all of you.

Bri, Bith, Erica, Ryan, and Tiffany, you are the best friends in the world. I am so lucky to have such talented, unique, and special friends in my life. I love all of you.

Joey, from being chased by an ax-wielding grandma fifteen years ago while on your four-wheeler, to cheering for the Tar Heels and competing in all different types of sports, I have thoroughly enjoyed having you as a friend.

Lloyd, thank you for teaching me to relax and have patience. . . . "That's some scurry stuff."

Sherry, I told you at graduation you were my scarecrow, and I meant it. You are so special to me and I feel fortunate to have such a dear friend in my life.

Candy, what you saw in me gave me strength to be who I am today. I am grateful.

Amanda, no matter what happens in my life, how mad we get at each other, or what we go through, I know you will always be there. You are more than my best friend, you are my sister.

Most important, to all of my former students, every day I spent with you was magic. I learned, I laughed, and I had the time of my life. Thank you from the bottom of my heart. I love you. —Mr. Clark

INTRODUCTION

Her name was Mudder. She loved *Guiding Light,* collards, and snuff, and she was my grandmother. Mudder stood right at five feet, but when she placed her hands on her hips, she was the tallest person in the room. She was definitely a lady who didn't put up with any nonsense, and she was respected by everyone around her; poor be the person who had to learn that the hard way. As I grew up, she lived with my family and had a strong impact on who I am today. She's one of the reasons that I feel so strongly about these fifty-five expectations I have of my students, as well as all people. She, along with my parents, gave me a true southern upbringing, which included respect, manners, and an appreciation of others. In addition to those ideals, I was shown how to enjoy life, take advantage of opportunities, and live every moment to the fullest. I was very fortunate to be surrounded by family members who were excellent examples of how life should be lived and not taken for granted.

Once I became a teacher, it became evident to me that many children aren't exposed to the type of guidance and opportunities that I had when I was growing up. I have tried to set an example for my students and be a role model like my family members were for me. In my attempt to give them an outline or a guide to how life should be lived and appreciated, I compiled this list of lessons. Over the years of working with kids and watching this list grow from five rules to a handbook of life's lessons, I have seen a remarkable difference in the way my students have held themselves, performed in school, and had respect for others.

I have used these lessons with much success with my students, but they are not only for children; most of the fifty-five items listed here can apply to anyone, young and old, from the housewife to the doctor, the politician to the waiter, and everyone in between. These lessons are about how we live, interact with others, and appreciate life, and, therefore, they speak to everyone.

I feel so fortunate to have had the opportunity to work with children firsthand and develop the list of fifty-five rules into what it is today. It is an extension of my upbringing mixed with lessons I have learned about life, along with some rules that I have felt the need to adopt in order to maintain order with my students and get them to achieve their potential. However, the rules are more than about getting kids to behave; they're about preparing kids for what awaits them after they leave my classroom. It is about preparing them to handle any situation they may encounter and giving them the confidence to do so. In some ways, it is a fifty-five-step plan. The steps, however, are not sequential; they are all explained, practiced, and enforced from day one in the classroom. At the end of the year, I like to say that my students are "polished." I know I can take them anywhere, put them in any situation, and present them with any lesson, because they are at a point where they are receptive to learning and eager to experience life.

The time I have spent with children and teaching them these lessons has been wonderful, and I can't imagine doing anything other than teaching. That is ironic, however, because when I was growing up, being a teacher was the last thing I would have wanted to do. Going through school, I can remember having aspirations of discovering ancient tombs in Egypt, flying around the world as a field journalist, or going undercover as a spy in foreign countries. The thought of entering such a dull, unchallenging, and mind-numbing profession as education never crossed my mind.

When I was a senior in high school, I sat down with my parents and discussed my options for college. Both of my parents were very hard workers, but it was still going to be a strain for them to come up with the funding necessary to send me to school. I can remember my father saying to me,

"Ron, that's not for you to worry about. That is our responsibility. You just concentrate on your grades." I loved them for the sacrifices they were willing to make for me, but I didn't want to put them in a situation where they would struggle to make ends meet. Around that time, I heard of a program called the Teaching Fellows Scholarship. Recipients of the award have all of their college expenses taken care of if they agree to teach in North Carolina for four years after graduating. I had no desire whatsoever to become a teacher, but I knew that taking the scholarship would make things much easier for my family financially. I decided I would use the funding to pay for my education, but after graduating I would not become a teacher. I would enter another profession that would allow me to make enough money to pay back the scholarship. It was not a plan I am proud of, but it made sense at the time.

Throughout college, I found that my one true love in life is adventure. I was up for any type of challenge that came my way, and that certainly led me to my share of wild moments. I once ran across the field of a nationally televised football game with my friend Bri, wearing only boxers and painted purple from head to toe, as we were chased by a gaggle of police officers in hot pursuit. While working at Dunkin' Donuts, and during a game of hide-and-seek, I hid in a warm, locked oven that was turned on, and because I had accidentally locked my coworker out of the building, I was almost cooked to death. Also, even though I am terrified of heights, I have bungee-jumped, climbed mountains, rappelled off cliffs, and parasailed behind a boat off the Atlantic coast. When I graduated from college, I realized I definitely did not want to teach. Actually, I didn't want to work at all. Therefore, in search of more adventures, I moved to London and worked as a singing and dancing waiter. After six months of using my southern accent as a British tourist attraction, I left England and backpacked across Europe, finally ending up in Romania, where I stayed with gypsies who fed me rat, which made me so sick that I had to be flown home. My adventures certainly had their share of highs and lows, but even when I ended up sick, almost cooked, or in trouble with the law, the experiences were worth the costs, because I always walked away a stronger, wiser, and better person.

After I arrived home from Romania, my parents were extremely happy to see me, but I had no intention of remaining home for long. My friend Bri was going to live on the beach in California, and I couldn't wait to move out there next. My mother, however, was willing to do whatever it took to get me to stay put. She told me of a fifth-grade teacher in our area who had recently passed away. It was a sudden illness, and her students, the faculty, and the entire community were affected by her loss. Now let me tell you, we live in the country, and the population of the town, Aurora, is about 600. You have to drive twenty minutes to get to a stoplight, and it is difficult to entice teachers to the school because of the travel it would require each day. Mom told me that substitute teachers had taken over the vacant teaching position for a month, and that the class had become very unruly. The school was about 75 percent minority and most of the kids were on free or reduced-price lunch. I felt sorry for the students, but I was not interested in taking over this class of demanding, high-energy fifth graders, many of whom had behavior problems and learning disabilities.

I told my mother there was no way in this world that I was going to teach at that school. She told me in return that if I didn't at least talk to the principal, she and my father would be forced to stop lending me money to fund my adventures. The next day, I was the first person to arrive at Snowden Elementary School.

Even though I agreed to meet with the principal, I still had no intention of taking the job. My Aunt Carolyn worked there as a secretary, so I figured it would give me the opportunity to see her before flying off to California. Upon arrival, I visited with my aunt, and then the principal, Andrea Roberson, gave me a tour of the school and told me about the group of students I would teach if I accepted the position. She told me about how demanding the students were, of several with learning disabilities, and how I *had* to raise those test scores no matter what. I remember thinking to myself, "And this lady is actually trying to convince me to work here." I did act interested, but my heart wasn't in it. She then escorted me to the room that held the fifth-grade class. We walked in and there was a little boy, named Rayquan, sitting just a few feet from the door. He looked up at me with his huge, brown, round eyes and said, "Is you gonna be our new teacher?" I can't explain the feeling that came over me; it was like an epiphany. The instant trust in his voice, the excitement all over his face, and his evident longing for stability called out to me. I knew that was where I was supposed to be. I looked back at Rayquan and said, "I think so."

Before taking over the class myself, the principal wanted me to observe the substitute teacher. She didn't want to just throw me in the class with no idea about what to expect from the group. The substitute in question, Mrs. Waddle, was an eccentric lady who always had a sandwich in one hand and whose matted wigs always seemed to lean to one side. On the first day I observed her, she became upset with a student who didn't know the answer to a question. She proceeded to draw three small circles in a row on the blackboard. She then instructed the young man to place his nose in the middle circle and one finger from each hand in the outside circles. She left him there and turned back to the class and asked the question again. The next student got the question right, and she threw her hands in the air and proclaimed that she felt the Holy Spirit. She then sang an entire verse of "Amazing Grace." Sitting there and watching this teacher for a week solidified more and more each day my desire to work with those students. They needed me more than I could have ever imagined. Before turning the class over to me, the substitute left me with one bit of "wisdom." She looked at me and said, "You know, Mr. Clark, you'll do fine. As long as you can affect the life of one child, you've been a success."

To this day I do not like that quote. I feel we have to approach education with the determination to affect each and every one of our students. The mentality of achieving "success" after reaching one child isn't enough. I approach each year with the knowledge that I have only one year to make a life's worth of difference in each child in that classroom, and I give it everything I've got. I didn't know much when I first entered the classroom and took over that class from Mrs. Waddle, but I did know my life was going to be different, because I was determined to give my students a different life, a better life. My time as a teacher had begun.

Over the next seven years in the classroom, my experiences were like a roller-coaster ride, with invitations to the White House, 911 calls, trips around the country with students, projects that garnered worldwide attention, and a major move from teaching in rural North Carolina to Harlem in New York City. Those events highlight my time spent working with children and my efforts to teach them these fifty-five rules. I have recounted many of the stories here. They show the highs and lows, successes and disappointments, and lessons learned along the way.

As you go through the list, there are some rules you may like and decide to use with students and children in your life, and there may be some that don't inspire you. We all have different levels of tolerance when it comes to the behavior of children, and we all have different levels of expectations for ourselves and others. I offer these rules as suggestions, as tried-and-true methods that have served my students well. I hope you find them useful.

★ RULE 1

When responding to any adult, you must answer by saying "Yes ma'am" or "No sir." Just nodding your head or saying any other form of yes or no is not acceptable.

Because I grew up in rural North Carolina, this one comes naturally to me, and it seems the obvious choice to come first. I feel it is one of the most important of all the rules, because it sets the tone for the type of respect I expect from my students. If you want children to respect you, you have to let them know it. Simply by telling them you want them to address you by saying "sir" lets them know the way you expect them to treat you. I also tell my students it's a very useful tool when dealing with adults, and furthermore it also comes in handy for any adult interacting with another adult. Case in point: I was on the phone recently with the phone company discussing the inaccuracies of my bill. The lady I spoke to was not helpful and seemed annoyed. Then, in the midst of the conversation, I threw in a "yes ma'am," and her entire attitude changed. She became far more helpful and easy to deal with, and she ended up cutting my bill in half, which was more than I had even asked for.

Some of my students in Harlem were interviewed for a chance to attend a high-rated junior high school. The school only had thirty openings for the following year, and twelve of my students were among the numerous kids across the city who applied for the spots. I practiced what the interview would be like with my students, and one main thing I stressed was, "Make sure you say 'yes ma'am' or 'no sir' no matter what!" Weeks after the interviews, I was delighted to hear that all twelve of my students had been accepted. When I talked with the admissions director at the school, the main comment he made over and over was how polite my students were in their interviews. It seems like just such a simple thing to do, but it gets results.

★RULE 2

Make eye contact. When someone is speaking, keep your eyes on him or her at all times. If someone makes a comment, turn and face that person.

Keeping eye contact is something that many people find hard to do, but it is important when you are trying to get your point across to people and show them you are serious about what you are saying. For example, if you go in to talk to your boss and ask for a raise, he is going to be far more likely to take you seriously if you are looking him in the eyes rather than glancing downward. If you are making a business proposal, people will be more likely to trust you and believe in your ideas if they see that you are confident, sure of yourself, and making eye contact with them.

I spend a lot of time encouraging my students to make eye contact. In order to give them practice, I put the kids in groups of two. I then tell them that making eye contact when you make a statement gives what you are saying more emphasis and emotion. When you look away or down at the floor, it shows you aren't sure of what you are saying and that you possibly aren't telling the truth. I also tell them that I have heard that repeated glances to the upper left-hand side mean you are being dishonest. Once they are in their groups, I have them practice talking to each other, taking note of how effective they are at maintaining eye contact with their partners.

Making eye contact is not only a way to show confidence, but it is also an important way to show respect. In class, when a student is expressing an opinion, I make sure all of the other students turn and are focused on that individual. I don't allow them to raise their hands to make additional comments until that person is finished, because, if they do, it looks as if they are more concerned with what they want to say than with the opinions of the speaker. I tell them to imagine what it would be like if they were trying to express a thought and everyone around them kept waving their hands. It would make them feel like their opinions had no value, and so, therefore, we don't do it.

I can remember when I was in school that it was awfully hard to daydream while staring at the teacher. If I could focus on the head in front of me or on my pencil, I was good to go, but watching the teacher just took something out of it. Therefore, I make sure to have all eyes on me at all times. That way, as I'm teaching I can see the looks on the students' faces and can tell if they are confused and lost or entertained and attentive. Also, since I am a very visual learner and teacher, I am constantly making motions with my hands and on the board, and I want the kids to follow along with me and know exactly where I'm coming from.

I have worked many a day in fast food. I've spent countless hours making the doughnuts at Dunkin' Donuts and waiting tables at various restaurants. Serving the public can be a thrill, but it can also be torture when you have to deal with difficult customers. I can remember how I always liked it when people would look me in the eyes to give their order. It is far more respectful to look a person in the face. As they were leaving, I always expected them to say thank you, but many didn't, and it baffled me. What were they thinking? Many who did say thank you just said it as they turned away or drove off. Why not take one second to look the person in the eyes and say thank you as if you mean it?

I try to get my students to practice doing this with various adults in the school who aren't teachers. Often custodians, cafeteria workers, secretaries, and teachers' aides aren't considered worthy of the respect teachers get, and I work hard to change that image in the minds of my students. I explain to the students the role of each person at the school and how his or her job makes it possible for kids to get a great education. I then tell them that people work harder and with more effort if they feel they are appreciated and that they are making a difference. I make sure I model the type of behavior I expect, as I interact with all members of the staff in a friendly and respectful manner. It doesn't take much effort before the students are following my lead, and the results are always obvious. When we go to the lunchroom, the students aren't allowed to talk in the line, and when they get their food, they must look the cafeteria workers in the eyes and say "May I" when asking for anything. In turn, they always thank the lunchroom workers and tell them to have a good day. The workers always comment on how wonderful the class is and how much they appreciate the respect.

No matter how we are interacting with others around

us and regardless of what we are saying, we will be taken more seriously and our actions will be much more appreciated if they come with eye contact.

★ RULE 3

If someone in the class wins a game or does something well, we will congratulate that person. Claps should be of at least three seconds in length with the full part of both hands meeting in a manner that will give the appropriate clap volume. (I know stating it that way makes me sound like a nut, but the kids love it.)

Think about a football or basketball game. What happens when someone scores a touchdown or makes a winning basket? The crowd goes crazy and cheers for that person. I think we should have that type of supportive environment and camaraderie in all areas where we have to work together to achieve goals, whether it be the workplace, the home, or especially the classroom. Any time people are given praise and rewarded for their efforts they are going to do a better job. That is obvious, but for some reason there are still parents who aren't cheering their kids on and principals and other leaders who just aren't creating the type of atmosphere where colleagues are celebrating each other's achievements.

I try to set the example for my students of how a real team and family would support and applaud others' efforts. On the first day of school, I give a speech that goes something like this:

> Is there anyone in here who doesn't like to be congratulated when they do something well? Of course not, we all do. Well, we are going to be a family this year, and families stick up for each other, they support each other, and they congratulate each other's successes. That is the type of environment we are going to have in this class, and, therefore, if someone does something well, let that person know. You can simply tell that person, "Good job," or you can applaud that person's efforts. How you do it doesn't matter, all that matters is that you make the effort to show appreciation for a job well done.

I then give the class examples of times when it would be appropriate to clap for other students. Sometimes it may happen after a good comment, a high test score, or an exceptional piece of writing. Also, if someone has a low score, we should still clap if that score shows improvement. We then go through a few role-playing exercises and practice clapping—yes, practice clapping. There can be no halfway clapping, as I call it. All of the students must clap in a way that shows respect and appreciation. Before I began to teach students how to clap, I would have half of the class clapping, a quarter of the class barely touching hands, and the rest of the class on some distant planet. After some detailed instruction, they were all on board.

Sometimes students start to clap for someone's comment or score that might not necessarily deserve applause. The rule is, if a few students start to clap, we will *all* start to clap. Apparently, those who started to clap saw something they appreciated. It would be far worse to have only a few weak claps than for us all to clap for something that might not be worthy.

As one teacher in a classroom that contained thirty-seven students, it was near impossible to give all of the students the attention and praise they deserved. It made it a lot easier when I had a classroom of students who were constantly looking to applaud each other's achievements. Acknowledgment from the teacher is always appreciated, but praise from a student's peers can have a much greater impact.

Teachers who visit my classroom always comment on how I have my students' grades posted around the room. This seems a bit unorthodox, because teachers are usually told to keep grades confidential in order to spare students' feelings. I have found that sharing the grades with the entire class can be a very positive experience, in the right type of environment. First of all, I don't post all grades—that would be impossible. I try to pick grades for assignments that all students, with effort, can do well on. Second, I try to pick assignments and grades that can be tracked over a period of time. For example, each night the students are given a reading assignment. The following morning, they are given a multiple-choice test (ten questions) on the assigned reading. I can grade the tests in less than five minutes, and I always have them ready to hand back on the same day. As I hand them back, I write the scores on a chart that will remain posted for the entire grading period. When I list the scores, I make a huge production out of it. I call the student's name, pause for a couple of seconds, and then I shout out the score—if it is 100, at the top of my lungs. The class cheers and the student's face lights up like crazy. A score of 90 will also receive claps and an 80 and sometimes even a 70 will receive claps if a student has shown improvement. The students love this, and they look forward to it all day.

Teaching and working in that type of environment is a positive experience and a lot of fun. I think people should try to recreate it in every classroom and workplace.

★ RULE 4

During discussions, respect other students' comments, opinions, and ideas. When possible, make statements like, "I agree with John, and I also feel that . . ." or "I disagree with Sara. She made a good

*point, but I feel that . . ." or "I think Victor made an
excellent observation, and it made me realize . . ."*

This is a rule I feel should be imposed in every board-
room and meeting in every workplace in America as well as
at every family dinner table. Too often we disregard the
comments of others and don't set the type of climate that
will allow people to speak freely and voice their thoughts
and opinions. All too often, people are worried about what
others will think of their ideas, and that they will be ridi-
culed or belittled and that their comments will be disre-
garded. I imagine there are hundreds of times every day
when the best idea in the room goes unheard or isn't even
voiced.

I knew I did not want that type of environment in my
classroom, so I developed a system with my kids that would
create a supportive and nonthreatening atmosphere. I wanted
to have more than just a class where students were allowed
to give their opinions; I wanted those thoughts and ideas to
develop into a discussion with a mutual appreciation for all
opinions. For this to happen, I found it was necessary to
teach the students, step-by-step, how to tell each other that
they agree or disagree with the other's comments in a respectful and supportive way.

The first thing I tell my students is that we will never
laugh or make fun of someone's comments. Every person in
the class has something to contribute, and in order for our

class to be the best it can be, we need to hear the opinions and ideas of everyone. I tell them it is okay to disagree, and that it is only human to not agree with everyone about everything. I point out, though, that there is a correct way and an incorrect way to let your feelings be known. We are each different, with different gifts, different experiences, and different roads that we have been down. There is no way to know all of the things that make up your neighbor's ideas. Therefore, we should just appreciate others' statements without being condescending or making them feel their way of thinking isn't right.

We practice this a great deal, and for many of the students, it is as if they are listening to one another's statements and taking value in what other people are saying for the first time. I can tell my students over and over how much I appreciate something they have said or that they made a very smart comment, but when a peer turns and says, "Wow, that was a great idea. I didn't think of that," it is valuable beyond words for that child's self-esteem and confidence. It is very similar to how it is wonderful to hear praise from our mothers, but it can mean more to us when those positive comments and acceptance come from our coworkers.

After a few months in Harlem, I began to see a difference in the students I was teaching, and it was evident to others as well. Individuals who would visit our school and observe my class always commented on how polite and supportive the students were of one another. They were amazed by how the students thoroughly enjoyed discussing ideas and how there was a mutual appreciation for all comments and opinions. I noticed the change firsthand in several ways. I remember that when I first started teaching in Harlem, I tried to get the students to teach me how to jump rope double-Dutch style. They weren't very supportive at first, and when I would make an attempt to jump the ropes, I didn't get any advice or extra tries. They would let me have just two attempts and then I would have to go to the back of the line.

I noticed that if you were good at jumping rope, all of the other students respected you; it was a major status symbol, and I knew that if I could do it, I would win points with the kids. I tried over and over, but every day they would just laugh at me. It seemed as if they didn't even want to give me the chance, because they knew it would take too much time and that I would never be able to do it anyway. Nevertheless, I was out there each day, trying it over and over. Oftentimes the ropes would hit me in the face and I would look awkward jumping all around trying to do it. The kids used to say that when I tried to double-Dutch I looked like a horse jumping up and down. Finally, after a few months, I started to notice a change in the kids. They started not only to become more supportive of one another in the classroom, but they were becoming more compassionate and caring outside the classroom as well. After three months of trying, I was just about to give up on ever being able to jump rope. One of the ropes actually slapped me on the forehead and I started to bleed. Mr. Clark's days of trying to jump rope were over; but then, the kids surrounded me and told me they believed in me and that I could do it. They started to turn the ropes slowly and talk me through it, giving advice and cheering me on. One girl said, "First, Mr. Clark, you've got to stop jumping like a horse. Jump like this." Every child wanted to show me his or her own technique, and it became obvious that they cared about my succeeding. One day, I went to jump in, expecting the usual slap in the face with the ropes, but something happened. I got in! I was actually jumping successfully between the ropes, and once I got in, I was in for good! I jumped for about thirty seconds straight screaming at the top of my lungs, "I'm in! I'm in!" All of the kids around the playground ran over to see, and they started cheering, "Go Mr. Clark! Go Mr. Clark!" The kids were as thrilled as I was and our relationship improved dramatically after that.

Often in class when I would try to teach difficult subject matter and the kids would feel they couldn't do it, I would say, "Now listen to me! You know . . . I didn't think I could double-Dutch, but you believed in me and you supported me, and I did it. Now, you don't think you can do this work, but I believe in you and I am here to show you I have faith in your ability, and know you will succeed." That really opened the kids' eyes. They often tell people, "Mr. Clark supports us when we need him, and we support him when he needs us, because he does need us sometimes and we teach him things too." Creating the type of environment where everyone supports each other and shows appreciation for the thoughts and abilities of others makes a world of difference in a classroom or in any other group of people who are trying to work together.

★RULE 5

If you win or do well at something, do not brag. If you lose, do not show anger. Instead, say something like, "I really enjoyed the competition, and I look forward to playing you again," or "Good game," or don't say anything at all. To show anger or sarcasm, such as "I wasn't playing hard anyway. You really aren't that good," shows weakness.

If you are good at something, others will recognize it. There is no need to tell others how talented you are, because by bragging about yourself, you are seen in a negative light, and people won't care about what skills you may have. This is obviously hard for many people to realize, because we seem to live in a culture where everyone wants to put their accomplishments and abilities on display. I used to be a huge fan of one certain movie/TV star/rapper. I thought he was extremely talented, and I enjoyed his work very much.

As of late, however, every time I see him on TV or read about him in magazines he is very cocky and makes statements to the effect that he is the greatest performer alive. It has really disappointed me so much and made me avoid paying to see anything that he is involved with. The shame is, everyone knows he is talented; there is no need for him to toot his own horn.

I don't want that to happen to my students, whether on a large scale or a small scale. No matter what their abilities, I want them to remain confident yet humble. Each year in North Carolina I would get my students involved in a basketball league, and at the end of each season the students would vote on the most valuable player. There was one boy named Draymond who was by far the best player. However, he felt the need to regularly remind everyone how good he was. After each season, he was so angry when he wouldn't be voted the most valuable player. The award always went to more humble players who truly appreciated playing on a team.

I tell my students that sometimes it is hard for people to stand back and not talk about their abilities, but if they can, it will make their skills seem much larger when they are realized by others. Draymond didn't need to tell everyone how good he was at basketball; that was obvious. He should have just focused on playing his heart out and let his performance speak for itself. That is the message I try to deliver to my students.

I also spend time talking to my students about how to lose gracefully. One of my biggest pet peeves is when someone loses a game and they say something like "I wasn't playing that hard anyway," or "I let you win that one."

My father, Ronnie Clark, is good at every type of competition you can come up with. He is great at darts, pool, horseshoes, cards, you name it. Occasionally, however, he has had the rare misfortune of losing to me. Granted, this doesn't occur often, but it does happen. I have always tried my hardest against him, but after each game that I won, he would always make comments like "Yeah, I took it easy on you that game," or "You didn't think I was trying, did you?" It used to drive me crazy! Now, after much frustration, we have a rule in our house and in my classroom: In any competition, we will always try our best, and will *never* make an excuse for why we lost to someone. It has made things so much nicer, and it has made playing a lot more fun and stress-free. It has almost gotten to a point where it doesn't matter who wins or loses, because we know that we are all trying our best, and we enjoy each other's efforts, no matter what the final outcome of the game.

★ RULE 6

If you are asked a question in conversation, you should ask a question in return. If someone asks,

"Did you have a nice weekend?" you should answer the question and then ask a question in return. For example:

Me: *"Did you have a nice weekend?"*

You: *"Yes, I had a great time. My family and I went shopping. What about you? Did you have a nice weekend?"*

It is only polite to show others that you are just as interested in them as they are in you.

This is a skill that takes a while to learn. Actually, I have met many adults who have yet to master it, and, in all honesty, many never will. I tell my students that when they are talking to someone, they should make sure not to monopolize the conversation. We have all encountered that person who just won't shut up, and I don't want any of my students to grow up to be that type of person. I want them to understand that you are far more likable and respectful when you are asking about the thoughts and opinions of others. It is simply an easy way to let someone know that you are interested in who they are and what they have to say.

When students walk in my classroom, I usually say something like, "Good morning, Terry, how was your weekend?" and he will respond, "Great, Mr. Clark, I went to the beach with my cousins." Then Terry would just run off to his seat. I always call the students back and tell them, "Hey, I just showed interest in what you did this weekend, and instead of showing me the same courtesy, you just ran off to your seat. Let's do that again. Terry, how was your weekend?" Terry will then respond, "Great, Mr. Clark, I went to the beach with my cousins. How was your weekend?" For kids, this takes a lot of practice, but the outcome is worth it.

Asking questions is also a skill that can come in handy when being interviewed. When my Harlem students went for their interviews to get into Manhattan East, an academically challenging junior high school, the admissions coordinator asked them who some of their favorite authors were. Many of my kids told me that after they named their favorites, they also asked the interviewer, "Do you have any authors you are particularly interested in reading?" It shows a higher level of consciousness on the part of the child and shows he is aware that the other person has interests, such as reading, as well. The same applies not just for interviews, but for any conversation.

This rule is about letting people know you are interested in them, and the results you will get when you do that. When I first started working at Snowden Elementary School in North Carolina, I made sure to spend time talking to my students about the things they were interested in. I asked them about their likes and dislikes and what they did for fun. I wanted them to know I cared about who they were, and that I wasn't there just to teach them out of a book.

I remember that in my first year of teaching there was a student named Jayson who was having a birthday party at his grandparents' trailer during the weekend. Jayson had invited me, along with almost every other teacher in the school, but when I asked around, I found out no other teacher was going. However, I told him I would be there, and I had kids asking me every five minutes if I was really going. That Saturday, even though I thought I had convinced them of my intentions, I don't think any of those kids expected me to pull up in that driveway. When I did, they all flooded around me like I was some kind of celebrity. We played freeze tag and hide-and-seek and had an incredible time. That day went a long way in terms of developing a relationship with the students and getting them to trust me. The next Monday, when I asked the kids to behave and pay attention, there was a different look in their eyes. They respected me, and they listened. There are many ways to show interest in others, from being an active listener and unselfish conversationalist to making special efforts to show others you care about them, but the bottom line is that it gets results.

★ RULE 7

When you cough or sneeze or burp, it is appro-priate to turn your head away from others and cover your mouth with the full part of your hand. Using a fist is not acceptable. Afterward, you should say, "Excuse me."

This one seems so simple, but it is surprising how many kids have never been told to do this. Actually, I notice adults all the time who cough and sneeze in public without placing a hand over the mouth. I absolutely hate riding the subway in New York during cold and flu season, because it is in-evitable that someone is going to stand right behind me and cough or sneeze on my neck. Once I watched a lady sneeze on a shorter lady standing beside her, and it was like one of those slow-motion commercials. Spit and vapor formed a cloud around her face and fell like a blanket on the shorter lady, and I can remember thinking to myself, "Have mercy, that poor woman has the flu now."

One important thing I point out to the kids is that after they sneeze or cough on their hand, they should wash their hands as soon as possible. Otherwise, they will be passing those germs along to everything and everyone they touch.

In order to help the kids remember this rule, I tell them about an old superstition that says that when you sneeze, evil spirits jump into your body. If you don't cover your mouth, the spirits will enter, but if you cover your mouth, you will keep them out. We say "God bless you" when someone sneezes, and in Germany you are supposed to say "Gesundheit." That means "Good health to you." Both expressions are said just in case you didn't cover your mouth in time and the spirits were able to enter your body. The kids love finding out the origins of these expressions and it inspires them to put the advice to use more often.

RULE 8

Do not smack your lips, tsk, roll your eyes, or show disrespect with gestures.

So much time and trouble is saved by getting this rule out of the way. I doubt there is a person in America who hasn't had someone smack their lips (the sound is also known as "tsk") or roll their eyes at him or her during one time or another. Kids, especially teenagers, love to do it, but I have been able to eliminate it entirely from my classes, just by pointing it out and making a rule that it will not happen in my classroom. On the first day of school, I ask if anyone in the class can smack their lips really well. I usually get more than a few students who are willing to demonstrate. I then get students to demonstrate rolling their eyes.

We then, as a class, combine the two, and we all smack and roll at the same time. It is usually a lot of fun, and I will always have a few students, the pros, who will turn in a good jerk of the neck and a few finger snaps. I talk to the students about how it is a form of disrespect, and that sometimes you don't have to say a single word in order to get yourself in a lot of trouble.

After that discussion, we are ready to role-play. I tell a student that I am going to reprimand her for not paying attention, and that I want her to smack her lips and roll her eyes. I tell her that I am then going to ask her to put her name on the board. We practice the exercise, and everyone understands why her name was placed on the board.

It makes it so nice when, a week later, I notice a kid smack and roll and I tell him to put his name on the board and I don't hear any arguments about it. Normally, if you try to punish kids for smacking their lips it is like putting gasoline on a fire. The smacks grow louder, the necks start jerking back and forth, and all hell is about to break loose. I let it be known that in my class even the smallest smack or roll of the eyes is going to be punished, and I stick to it.

There was one girl, named Shamitha, in Harlem who had what I call the smacking disease. If she had to put her name on the board for any reason, a smack was going to slip out. It was like an involuntary action, and she didn't even realize she was doing it. I would say, "Okay, now add a check," and another smack would come out. This would usually go on until she had detention, but, even then, she never got angry, because she knew it was against a rule and she knew she shouldn't be doing it.

My first year teaching I taught a little girl named Antoinkena who was one pistol. Her hair was pulled straight up into a point on the top of her head and she had eyes as big as walnuts. She was the shortest girl in the class, but she had a forceful presence, and all of the other students were afraid of her, and I think some of the teachers were as well. She was definitely a handful, and her trademark was smacking her lips and rolling her eyes. I was still very new at dealing with kids, and so when she smacked her lips and rolled her eyes at me, I did the only thing that came to mind; I took one hand and pulled all of my hair up into one point, I sucked in my lips like a fish, and I rolled my eyes right back at her. That might not have been the best way to handle that situation, but Antoinkena sure froze like stone, and I definitely got her attention. She just looked at me in shock for a minute, and then I smiled, and she smiled, and then we started laughing. In dealing with Antoinkena and kids like her, sometimes it takes some unusual actions to get their attention and get them to behave. By imitating her action, it somehow worked, and I never had to deal with her smacking her lips at me again. I guess she knew that if she did, I was just going to throw it right back at her.

Although that tactic worked with Antoinkena, it obviously wasn't the best way to handle the situation. Making sure the kids know exactly what is expected of them in terms of their gestures and attitude, and making sure they are aware of the consequences for those behaviors, is the best way to avoid those actions.

RULE 9

Always say thank you when I give you something. If you do not say it within three seconds after receiving the item, I will take it back. There is no excuse for not showing appreciation.

In my opinion, this one is major. I cannot tell you the countless times I have had to take things away from students who forgot to say thank you. They're always surprised at the beginning of the year at what happens when I am handing out cookies at lunch or homework passes and students forget to say thank you. I take the item back, and they honestly believe I am just joking and that I'm going to wait a few seconds and then give them a second try. It never happens. In order for this rule to work, you have to enforce it, and sometimes that is difficult. Once, a student, along with four other kids, won a set of books for having the highest score on a social studies test. The little girl was so excited that she was jumping up and down. Others in the class quickly pointed out that she forgot to say thank you, and I had to take the books away from her. It broke my heart, but once I went with the rule, I wouldn't turn back; I had to remain consistent. The kids understood that and rarely complained when I had to take things away from them. They knew it was a rule, and I had stated explicitly the way it worked from day one.

I recently talked with a twelfth-grade teacher at a local high school in North Carolina. She walked up to me and said she had been wanting to meet me for some time. She said she often gives treats or rewards to her seniors, and that there was a group of boys in her class who always made a point to say thank you. She said that one day she commented on how polite they were, and that they told her they *had* to be polite because their fifth-grade teacher drilled it into them. She said one boy recalled how one day in fifth grade he had won a lollipop, but before he could put it in his mouth Mr. Clark had taken it away because he hadn't said thank you. He said Mr. Clark then put the lollipop in his own mouth and with a big grin he went back to teaching. That had stuck in his mind, and he swore he would never forget to say thank you again.

In my day-to-day life, I always try to make sure to thank whoever I am dealing with—the checkout clerk, the waitress, a person who holds the door for me, the friend who does a favor, or anyone who does something for me, no matter how major or minor. At my school in Harlem, the custodian would occasionally mop and clean our rooms during the night shift. I was always so pleasantly surprised when I walked into my freshly cleaned room, and I would make a point to thank him several times for doing such good work. He always seemed surprised that I was thanking him for just doing his job. I could tell he appreciated it, though, and I started to notice that my room was being mopped and cleaned a lot more often.

When I would take the subway to work in New York City, Monday mornings meant that I had to stand in a long line to get my week's worth of tokens. The token lady at my subway stop always looked like she had just swallowed a lemon, and I hated having to deal with her first thing every Monday morning. She would *never* speak to anyone, she would just have this grimace on her face, take the money, and shove the tokens toward the customers. Well, I was determined I was going to get her to be nice to me. Each and every Monday morning, I said to her, "Good morning," with no response. I would then end with "Thank you," and again, there would be no response. I kept at it, however, even though on the inside I just wanted to say, "Excuse me, are you aware that you are the rudest person on earth?" One day, after several weeks of this, when I said "Thank you," she replied, "You're welcome." I almost fell out. The next person in line approached the window to order, but I jumped back and said, "What did you say?" She looked shocked, and she said, "You're welcome," and she smiled at me. From then on, my Monday morning subway experiences were pleasant . . . well, as pleasant as a Monday morning subway experience can be.

★ RULE 10

When you are given something from someone, never insult that person by making negative comments about the gift or by insinuating that it wasn't appreciated.

One month I took all of the top readers in the class to a Charlotte Hornets pro basketball game. They got to stay overnight in a hotel, meet the players, and have a blast at the game. The following month, the top readers were going to be rewarded with a trip to the local bowling alley. The disparity is hard to miss, and it definitely didn't go unnoticed by the students. They were vocal about the difference in the trips, and it really hurt my feelings. Most teachers weren't taking their students on any trips at all, yet mine were complaining that the bowling trip wasn't nice enough. In order to teach them a lesson, I canceled the bowling trip and gave them no reward. It may seem harsh to cancel the trip, but it was a very effective way to get my point across to the ungrateful students, and hopefully the memory of why they were punished will be a lasting one.

It's irritating to give a gift that's not appreciated. It may not be surprising that my little nephew, Austin, has a problem with being gracious. My sister and her husband adopted him from the Ukraine, and when he first arrived here at the age of four, he was so appreciative of everything. When he was given a present, he would carefully remove the wrapping paper and fold it ever so carefully and place it to the side. He would then gently open the box to see what was inside. His face would always light up, and he would hug whatever was in the box—socks, books, shirts, you name it. He has been here over a year now, and things have changed quite a bit. I often give him presents, but lately I have been giving him more clothes than anything else. Now, when he opens the presents, he rips into them with wild abandon (well, I can't blame him for that; that is the fun part), but when he sees that the present is clothes, he frowns and says, *"Uncle Rooooooonnnnnnnn!"* as if I should have better sense than to buy something so boring. I guess all kids *feel* that way, but out of respect for whoever has given them a gift or some sort of reward, it is important to teach them not to *act* that way. I am working with Austin on that, but at the age he is now, it is going to take some practice. The last few clothing presents I gave him, however, he did respond by saying, "Uncle Ron, I just love it." He is learning.

★ RULE 11

Surprise others by performing random acts of kindness. Go out of your way to do something surprisingly kind and generous for someone at least once a month.

All of the kids love this rule, and it sounds as if it is a really good idea and that it would be a lot of fun. The problem is that it is one of the hardest of the rules for people to follow. In our daily lives, we get so busy and preoccupied that there isn't much time to sit down and think up a surprise for someone. Usually, if it isn't someone's birthday or a special occasion, people really don't see a need to go out of their way to do something special for someone else. I feel, however, that the best time to give someone a nice surprise is when it isn't expected. That way, the person knows you didn't do it because of obligation, you did it because you wanted to.

The types of surprises I'm talking about are more than just getting someone a gift. These surprises need to be more thought-out and meaningful. For example, take the time to make a lunch, complete with salad, entrée, and dessert, and set it up in a room where you work. Place flowers on the table and play some soft music in the background. Then invite the custodians to take a break and enjoy the lunch you prepared for them. Or, when your neighbors are at work, mow their lawn and clip their hedges. I tell my students that they can clean their entire room, vacuum the house, or do the dishes, without being asked to. They can do errands or read to an elderly neighbor or they can take someone fresh flowers. The opportunities are all around.

The reason behind my desire to surprise others stems from how my parents were constantly arranging surprises for my sister and me. I remember how seeing them go out of their way to do kind and unexpected things for us made me feel so special and loved. I promised myself that when I was older I was going to do similar things for all of those around me. When I became a teacher, I found myself spending hundreds of dollars a month on books, contest prizes, and many other items for the students. Small surprises like that were appreciated by the kids, but then something happened. I started a project with the kids that led to the biggest surprise I had ever been involved with. It forever changed my life and the lives of the students.

It all started when I was teaching a lesson on the newspaper, and the students were having trouble understanding how the classified ads work. I decided to have them place their own ad in the paper so they could see firsthand how the process works. I had each child bring a nickel to contribute to the ad, because I wanted to give them ownership in the project. I then instructed them to come up with an ad for the classifieds. Immediately, they wanted to place a Lexus for sale in the Autos For Sale section, but then I had to remind them, "We don't have a Lexus!" Finally, we decided to place a geography puzzle in the paper and ask readers to write us back with the answer. Our first puzzle stated: "What is the largest island in the world? If you know the answer, please write to our class." We included our address and anxiously waited to see if we would get a response. To our surprise, we received ten letters from different individuals around the area. The kids loved it, because no one had the right answer, and they got to write each person back with the correct answer, Greenland.

The kids were so excited with the letters we received that we decided to place additional puzzles in papers across the state. The project became less about a lesson on the classifieds and more about what the students were learning from all of the people who were writing our class. In order to get more responses, we marched in parades with banners that had questions painted on them along with a request to send answers to our school. We passed out flyers at local supermarkets and even gave a puzzle on a radio show. Soon we were receiving dozens of letters a day from people across our state—doctors, lawyers, Arabian horse farm owners, people from all kinds of professions. My students in our small town of 600 people were learning about life outside of our town. The whole process was essential for these kids who had very little experience of life beyond their community.

The kids were thoroughly enjoying the project, when one day a boy named Luke said, "Hey, Mr. Clark, I was thinking, we should go *worldwide* with this project." He meant that we should put a puzzle in a paper that goes all around the world. It sounded like a good idea to me, so I decided to send Luke to the office to call *USA Today* in order to find out how much a 4 × 5-inch ad would cost in their paper. It has always bothered me when I call my students' homes and they have poor phone manners, so I try to get my students to make calls for me whenever possible. I made sure Luke knew precisely what I wanted him to ask on the telephone and exactly what information I expected from him. I then demonstrated a practice call with him, in front of the other students, and then I sent him to make the call. When Luke returned, he placed his hands on his hips and informed me seriously in his deep southern drawl, "Mr. Clark, you better sit down." He proceeded to tell me that it was going to cost $12,000. I didn't believe him at first, and I had to call myself after school to confirm the amount. I found out that Luke was right, and I was astounded at how much such a little ad would cost for just one day's printing in the paper.

After much discussion with the kids, I explained to them that it would be impossible for us to raise that amount of money. The students, however, were not willing to give up so easily. They begged me to let them try, and soon we began a campaign to raise the necessary funds. I told them I would do any fund-raiser they were interested in: bake sales, candy sales, *anything* but a car wash, because I hate car washes. That Saturday, we had a car wash.

Weeks later, our "creative" earning strategies weren't getting us very far, when I received a phone call from *USA Today*. An editor for the paper, Joan Baraloto, told me that someone had seen my class on TV trying to raise the money, and that he wanted to donate the $12,000 necessary for the ad. I immediately asked her the name of the person, and she told me he wanted to be known only as "Santa Claus." It was three weeks before Christmas, so it seemed to be a fitting title for such a generous contributor. I hurried to the class and informed the kids that someone had donated the money for our ad. They cheered like crazy and then asked, "Who gave us the money?" I replied with a slight grin, "Santa Claus." Luke looked at me incredulously and said, "Mr. Clark, my parents ain't got that kind of money."

We eventually decided to place the following ad:

ATTENTION PRESIDENT CLINTON AND PEOPLE AROUND THE WORLD
What kills more people each year than AIDS, alcohol abuse, car accidents, murders, suicides, illegal drugs, and fires combined?

The students actually created this ad, and I was a little worried about it, because coming from a state that produces so much tobacco, I didn't want to ruffle any feathers. I mentioned that to the kids, and one girl, Carmela, said to me, "Well, Mr. Clark, just because we come from this state doesn't mean we can't have our own opinions." She had a point.

We placed our address and fax number in the ad, and anxiously awaited the responses. Unfortunately, coming from such a rural school, we didn't have e-mail at that time and couldn't include an Internet address.

On the day the ad appeared, I wasn't even able to get a paper because *USA Today* isn't delivered to our rural area. The effects of the ad were felt, however, as we had already received over a hundred faxes before I even arrived at school. As I pulled into the parking lot of the school, my mild-mannered co-teacher, Barbara Jones, was in the parking lot jumping up and down and cheering, "Mr. Clark, Mr. Clark, you've got to get to the office! Stop the car, I'll park it for you!" As I ran into the office, the first fax I picked up and read was from the Prime Minister of Canada. There were also faxes from the cast of *Friends*, sports teams, doctors in Bombay, India, and people from everywhere you can imagine.

When the students arrived at school, we took over the office! Radio shows all over the country were reading our ad on the air and asking their listeners to call in with their answers. The radio shows were then calling our school to find out what the real answer was, so there were kids on three different phone lines talking to thousands of listeners. I had kids out in the hall being interviewed by TV reporters, faxes coming in constantly from all over the world, and students about to jump through the roof with excitement! When the school day was finally over, we realized that the fax machine was going to be going all night, and that no one would be there to keep paper in the machine, and that we would lose a lot of responses; therefore, I had to spend the night in the school office. Faxes came in constantly throughout the entire night. Around 3:00 A.M. I got one that said, "MR. CLARK, CALL US!" and a number was attached. I called, and it was a casino that had posted the question and was taking bets on the answer. They were calling me to confirm the correct answer so they could pay out the winners. It was WILD!

It was so much fun to learn about the various individuals and to hear all of their responses to our question. Here are some of our more common and favorite responses: starvation, guns, falls in the tub, James Bond, love, heart attack, abortion, old age, suspense, ignorance, the fifth grade, time, greed, the tongue, hangnails, puzzles.

We eventually received over 7,000 letters and packages from all over the world. We had promised in the ad to write each person back, so the kids had to meet on Saturdays, during holidays, and after school in order to hand-write each individual a response, letting each person know that the correct answer is tobacco use.

The students were becoming local celebrities, being featured on national news programs and on the covers of newspapers across the state. A great deal of excitement surrounded the project, and the kids were starting to hold their heads high and come to school each day on top of the world.

After a week of writing letters, turning the school office into our own makeshift headquarters, and being the center of media attention, we finally received the answer we had been waiting for. The White House called and said that Hillary Clinton would be calling on Friday at 11:45 A.M. to give the President's and her answer and to discuss the dangers of tobacco use with the students. We were all elated, and rushed to set up a press conference for the end of the week so that all of the community could be in attendance for the call.

As we all sat in the library, political leaders, business owners, family, and friends, you could just feel the excitement in the air and the sense of community. We had purchased clothes so that all of the students were dressed in "Sunday clothes" and looking their best. The class and I sat at tables at the head of the library with dozens of cameras and media personalities only a few feet from our faces. I looked at the clock . . . 11:43 . . . I looked again . . . 11:44. . . . Then I thought, "What if this woman doesn't call?" Then it rang.

The library is supposed to be quiet, but it had never been that quiet. We all held our breath as we hung on every word of the call, which was supposed to be fifteen minutes but stretched to forty-five minutes in length. Mrs. Clinton took the time to speak with each child individually and to discuss the health issues raised by our question. At the end of the call, Mrs. Clinton said, "You know, I've got this letter here that the President and I wrote to your class that includes our answer, and we could mail it to you, but we would much rather give it to you in person." Then I made an announcement that shocked everyone. I had been talking with the White House all week, and we had arranged for the students to actually go to the White House the following week to meet with the First Family. This was going to be a life-changing event for the students, as most of them had never even left our state. When we were first informed about the ensuing invitation to the White House, the principal asked me not to make the trip public knowledge until I had enough funding to take all of the students. We knew it was going to take quite a bit of effort. Immediately, Mrs. Austin, one of the secretaries at the school, and I began calling every business we could think of to try to get donations. I discovered quickly that no matter who I called, they were interested in helping kids and were willing to contribute to helping in any way they could. I have found that true no matter where I have taught; communities are willing to help teachers, as long as you can show you are hardworking and can give solid reasons for how the contributions can make a difference.

Luckily, within a few days funding for the entire trip had been obtained from local business owners, all of whom had agreed to keep the secret until it was announced at the press conference. At the end of the phone call, in response to Mrs. Clinton's request for us to go to the White House, I said, through tears that I could not suppress no matter how hard I tried, "Kids, you see this community of business leaders around you . . . well, they have been kind enough to make contributions to our class, and next week WE'RE ALL GOING TO WASHINGTON, D.C.!!" The library erupted with applause. I was crying, the students and their parents were crying, Sandra Harris from Channel 9 was crying. Delivering that surprise to those students and that community was one of the most amazing moments of my life. The joy, excitement, and appreciation on the faces of those students is one of the main reasons I decided to continue teaching. How could I turn my back on the opportunity to have that kind of an impact on the lives of children?

After the excitement of the announcement calmed

down, I began to organize the trip. I expected it was going to be overwhelming, but once I started making calls, obtaining hotel reservations, and jotting out an itinerary, everything just seemed to fall into place. It does take effort for such an undertaking, but I just relied on the advice of those around me whom I trusted, and I made sure I tried to cover every possible detail.

The following week we made the trip to D.C., along with reporters from local newspapers. We visited the National Symphony Orchestra, the Capitol building, and all of the major museums. The last day of our time in D.C. we made our trip to the White House. A guide gave us a personal tour, and we were the only ones there at the time. We were allowed to roam free, take pictures, and make ourselves at home. One of the highlights of the visit was the bathroom, because the toilet tissue had a picture of the White House on every sheet. Later, when we left, Mrs. Jones said, "I wanted to take one of those rolls of tissue," and Mr. Farrow, a parent, smiled as he pulled one out of his bag.

After our tour, we were led to the East Room; it was decorated with a huge Christmas tree with lights everywhere. Finally, the President and Mrs. Clinton entered the room and began talking to the kids. President Clinton read the students " 'Twas the Night Before Christmas," and then we all sang Christmas carols. When we were done, the President actually knelt on the floor to talk to each child and

Mrs. Clinton went around and talked to the adults. When she walked over to me, she said, "Oh, Mr. Clark, I recognize you from the newspapers," and I replied, "Oh, Mrs. Clinton, I recognize you from TV."

When the kids and I got back to North Carolina, they didn't want the project to end. In order to keep it alive a little longer, we wrote a book about the entire project called *An Adventure Around the World Through the Words of Others.* The students had so many feelings and memories tied in with that project, and I feel so fortunate that we were able to capture those feelings in time by collecting them all and placing them in writing. I know twenty years from now some of them will read the book to their children, and hopefully those emotions will come to life again.

That was a once-in-a-lifetime experience, but I was lucky enough to have a similar experience with my students in Harlem. Each year, Disney sponsors the American Teacher Awards. In my second year in New York City, I found out I was a finalist for the Outstanding Teacher of the Year award and that I was supposed to fly to Los Angeles in November for the final stages of the competition. I told the people at Disney that I would really love to bring my class with me. They informed me that Disney could not help me financially, but that if I could raise the money I was more than welcome to bring my students.

I didn't want to get the students' hopes up, so I didn't

tell them what I was trying to do. Instead, I went around to businesses throughout New York City and I wrote over a hundred letters to business owners. Thanks to the efforts of students' parents and the assistant principal, Mrs. Castillo, who spent days on the phone arranging funding and finding sponsors, and a lot of hard work, small amounts of money started to come in. Then, one day I got a phone call from a student's mother, Mrs. Miriam Vazquez, who told me that the law firm where she worked, Morrison and Foerster, was so touched by the attempt to take all of the students on the trip that they were going to contribute the remaining $16,000 needed to make the trip possible! I was thrilled! I immediately called a night meeting for all of my students and their parents in the auditorium. I told them that we had raised enough money so that a few students could go on the trip and that we were going to put all of their names in a fishbowl and draw out the names of the three lucky students. I said to the group, "As you know, I am going to Los Angeles next month, and you have all been very wonderful and supportive. Well, I want you to know that when I go, I won't be alone. We have received enough donations so that I will be taking a few very special students with me, and we are here tonight to determine who they will be. As you see I have this fishbowl with all of your names in it." I then placed my hand in the bowl and started to twirl the names around, and you could just see the anticipation on all of the

fers from the actual grade will be deducted from your
paper. The only marks you are allowed to make on
others' papers are an "X" and the number they got in-
correct.

As adults, we are always put in situations where we have to look at the performance of others and make judgments. We do it constantly on the job, whether we are interviewing candidates, evaluating our coworkers, or choosing our business partners. We are able to learn a lot about ourselves and the level of achievement we should expect from ourselves by observing the way our peers operate. Assessing others and letting them know your summation of their abilities can be very challenging, however, because you must have a great deal of confidence in yourself in order to do so. You must feel secure with your own performance before you can tell others what is right or wrong with how they have performed. Teaching students to evaluate the work of their peers in the classroom, and having them practice appropriate techniques of delivering feedback, will prepare them for what they are going to face later in life.

Unfortunately, some school systems do not allow students to grade each other's papers because it can be a social embarrassment for students who aren't doing well. If not done under the right supervision and in the right type of classroom environment, I agree with that sentiment. As I discussed earlier, however, if you create a supportive atmosphere where students feel comfortable with others knowing their scores, then the sharing of grades can be very helpful and go a long way toward motivating students.

First of all, having students grade each other's papers is quick and offers immediate feedback to the teacher. The main problem is that students' feelings may be hurt; therefore, I often have the students leave off their name on their papers. After I teach a lesson, I have the students take out a sheet of paper. I then ask them anywhere from five to ten questions, and I have them pass up their papers. I immediately turn around and pass the papers back out, so that no one knows exactly whose paper they have. I give the answers, and then I have the students raise their hands for perfect scores, minus one, minus two, and so on. This gives me a good, and immediate, indication of the class's mastery of what I have taught. Having the students grade each other's papers, therefore, served its purpose and didn't embarrass any of the students. For times when no names have been placed on papers, I just collect them back from the students and chuck them in the trash; there is no need to keep them around, because I already got the feedback I needed.

There are times, however, when I want to have a more specific idea of how each child is doing, so I do have the

students write their names on the papers. After they have
been checked, I have the students hold on to the papers
they checked. I then ask them to raise their hands to designate the number of questions missed before they pass
the papers back. This spares a student the humiliation of
having to raise her own hand to show that she has a low
score.

Sometimes, I have students who graded a paper with a
perfect score call out the names of the individuals who performed so well.

Before you have a class grade papers with the names on
each paper, there are two things I would make sure to discuss:

#1. Tell the students that privacy is required at all times
when grading someone else's paper. Tell them they are
not to comment on the other student's grade, not to
that student or any other student in the class.

#2. When grading, the students are only to mark X's for
incorrect answers and a final tally at the top of the paper
showing how many were wrong. This is important, because you will have some students who will get carried
away and write things on the papers like "You go girl!"
or "Lord knows you did bad," or "What were you thinking?" Those are all actual comments I have seen stu-

dents write on papers in the past. Limiting what they can put on the paper will also keep them from being able to change answers. If you are going over the answers with the class and you see a student writing words, you will know something is up because there is no reason for them to be writing anything on the paper other than an "X."

⭐ RULE 13

When we read together in class, you must follow along. If I call on you to read, you must know exactly where we are and begin reading immediately.

I can remember sitting in classes, as a student, while we read together as a group. Sometimes, out of boredom, I would stare at the page we were on and daydream about anything from winning the lottery to being asked by NASA to be the first high school student to fly to the moon. I seldom paid attention to the details of the text, but I always managed to get the general gist of what was being read. It just didn't excite me enough to command my full attention.

As an adult, I would find myself in numerous meetings where I had that same type of boredom, and I would just shut down and not pay attention to what was going on. In order to get through it, I had to force myself to be an active participant. I would think of questions to ask, make comments, and take notes. I tried to make the most of the time I had to spend in any particular meeting, because I was going to have to be there anyway. Many times, I would not even have the opportunity to make my comments or ask my questions, but just getting in the mind-set that I might be speaking or raising my hand at any second put me in a different frame of mind. My heart would race a little faster and I would pay attention. I try to get my kids to learn to be active participants in that way. I try to get them to stay on task, following along in the books we are reading and preparing themselves to make comments or ask questions throughout the lessons. No one in my class is going to slouch down and stare out the window. We will all stay focused and be part of the lesson and discussions.

When reading together, having everyone on task and attentive at all times can be unrealistic and almost impossible to achieve. I have found that the subject students find most boring is reading. Some students just absolutely hate it; especially silent reading. I was once reading a chapter of *The Indian in the Cupboard* with my class, and I stopped and asked them to continue reading silently. I turned and began writing the homework on the board, and I felt that someone was standing behind me. I turned and there was a little boy named Drew looking up at me with a very content expression. I said, "What is it, Drew?" and he said, "I finished that reading, Mr. Clark." Drew wasn't a very good reader, and I knew there was no way he could have finished the entire chapter. I said, "You did!" and he said, grinning from ear to ear, "Yep, I read the *whole* page." I just looked at him, raised an eyebrow, and said with a smirk, "Now, Drew . . ." and he replied in an embarrassed way, "Oooooh, I'm sorry, Mr. Clark, you wanted us to read the front AND the back of the page," and he turned and trotted off to his seat. I didn't have the heart to tell him I expected him to finish reading the whole chapter.

My point of mentioning my daydreaming in high school and Drew's misunderstanding is that reading and staying on task can be a real struggle. I mean, you are going to have students who just love to read. They are going to be attentive with little effort on the part of the teacher. It is the students who dread reading and have difficulties with it that I try to reach when doing reading with my class. There are several strategies I use together with my rule about following along as we read as a class.

Strategy 1

When I read with my students, I read with force, energy, and expression. I try to let go of all inhibitions and "become" the character. Sometimes while reading I'll jump on a student's desk, jump over to another desk, scream at the top of my lungs, or fall to the floor. Anything I can do to make the reading more dramatic and to take the students to that place in the story, I do it. I have a thousand different voices that I use, and there are times when I will finish part of a reading passage and the kids will just break into applause. They genuinely appreciate my efforts to bring the readings to life and to make the story exciting. The way I read transfers to my students as well, as they, too, read with expression and have character voices of their own. It makes the whole experience more enjoyable, and it teaches them how captivating reading can be.

Strategy 2

I try to select novels and readings that I think are enchanting, appealing, and full of intriguing characters. One of the main tests I use when selecting readings is to ask myself if it is something I would enjoy reading. If the answer is no, I pick something else. I hear kids all the time talk about how they don't like to read. I always tell them that perhaps they just aren't reading the right things.

Strategy 3

This is where Rule 13 takes effect. I think that if the readings I have selected are entertaining and if we are reading them as a class with energy and expression, then the students have no reason not to pay attention as we are reading. Therefore, I have the rule that if I see that a student's eyes are not on the page as we are reading, or if I call on a student to read and he or she doesn't know where we are, that child's name will be placed on the board. In the beginning, I always have to place several names on the board. Some students prefer to watch my facial expressions rather than follow the words on the page, and it takes a while to teach them to "see" the story in their minds. Also, there is a time set aside each day when I read to the kids out of a novel, and they aren't required to follow along. That helps them develop their listening comprehension skills and gives them the opportunity to "watch the show."

Why is it so important to have the students follow along when we are reading together? First of all, as we read, they are seeing new words and hearing their pronunciations, which adds to their word recognition and vocabulary base. It also helps them to observe the appropriate rhythmic flow of text. Most important, however, I am training them to learn to focus as they read and comprehend as they go along.

★ RULE 14

Answer all written questions with a complete sentence. For example, if the question asks, "What is the capital of Russia?" you should respond by writing, "The capital of Russia is Moscow." Also, in conversation with others, it is important to use complete sentences out of respect for the person's question. For example, if a person asks, "How are you?" instead of just responding by saying, "Fine," you should say, "I'm doing fine, thank you. How about yourself?"

This rule helps students to develop a command of the written language. It helps them learn to develop and organize their thoughts, especially when the questions require a short but thought-out answer. For example, the question "Do you feel the proposal to add forty-five minutes to the school day should be passed?" might be answered with a no without any explanation unless kids are taught to answer their questions in depth and with complete thoughts.

My co-teacher in North Carolina, Barbara Jones, taught math and science, but she did a wonderful job of integrating writing into her subjects. She had her students keep a math journal, and in it they would explain, in writing, the way they solved various problems. She always asked that they begin their answer by restating the question and using complete sentences. This was an excellent way to integrate subjects, and, as the students' writing teacher, I appreciated the extra effort she took to work with them on their writing skills.

Each year in North Carolina the fifth graders are given an open-ended assessment test. They are asked to read a passage and then respond to short-answer questions about the text. At times, I had nonreaders and students far below grade level in my class. When working on writing, however, I would always instruct them to answer their questions in the following way:

(This is a brief outline of the technique.)
Example question:

Of the basketball players, who do you think was better, Lloyd or Jason?

1. Restate the question and give your answer:
   Of the basketball players, I think that Lloyd was better.

2. Give a reason why you feel that way:
   I think Lloyd was better because he made the winning shot.

3. Support your answer:
   Since he made the winning shot, that shows that he stayed calm under pressure and that he was determined to win.

4. Restate the question and close.
   Therefore, I think that Lloyd was a better player than Jason.

. . . . . .

After much work and development of that basic outline, my students soon learned to write well-developed, thought-out answers to any question. After mastering this technique, many of my students were able to use this outline to write more creative and elaborate answers, but their answers retained the organization needed to make their writing top-notch. Even my nonreaders found the outline easy to learn and they found success with it as well.

In my first year, I had only been with the class three weeks before the open-ended test, and many of the non-readers just sat and stared at the test and wrote nothing. It broke my heart, but all I could do was smile and tell them to try their best. I taught both fifth-grade classes at the school, and we scored dead last in the county on the test in my first year of teaching. The next year, I was determined that our scores would rise. I developed the writing outline, and we worked on it throughout the year in all subjects. When the test results came back, every fifth grader at my school passed the test, and our school scored first in the county. I even had students who were reading on a first-grade level pass the test, because they had learned to restate the question, give an answer, give support to that answer, and restate for a closing.

★ RULE 15

At times throughout the year, I will give rewards for good behavior, academic performances, and other acts worthy of praise. If you ever ask me for a reward, however, it will not be given. It is rude to ask if you are getting something for good behavior. You should be good and try your best because you are trying to better yourself, not because you are anticipating a reward. I usually give some sort of reward to everyone who scores 100 on unit tests. If you make 100 and ask if you are getting something, no one who made 100 will be given anything.

At work in the real world, rewards aren't always given to people for a job well done. People do a good job because they take pride in their performance, they love what they do, and/or they want to keep their jobs. Even though I reward my students often, I know that I have to prepare them for what life is going to be like after the classroom. I try to get them to perform and realize it is important to do well not for a reward but for themselves.

I really go out of the way to reward my students and praise them for their work, but it got to a point where I felt as if the kids were going from being appreciative for the things I was giving them to a point where they'd say, "What are we getting next?" Once I passed reports back to the class, and a little girl who got the highest grade said, "Mr. Clark, am I getting anything?" From that moment on, I put an end to comments like that. I made sure that the class understood that under no circumstances were they ever to ask me for any type of reward or if they were getting anything. The students still might have felt a bit greedy on the inside, but I was going to make sure that at least their actions did not reflect it. Over time, I hoped that learning to accept what is given without expecting and asking for rewards would sink in and change their attitudes toward the benefits of a good, individual performance.

Even after I told the students this rule, they would occasionally still slip up. One time I stayed up late making homemade chocolate chip cookies for the kids who would pass the next day's unit test on the Revolutionary War. After I passed back the tests, Queshida said, "Mr. Clark, do we get anything for doing good on the test?" You could have heard a pin drop in the class. There were big eyes all over the classroom, and mine were the biggest! I was livid, because I had stayed up for hours making those darn cookies . . . okay, it took me five minutes to slice them off the roll, but nevertheless, I knew that I couldn't give them out after she had asked for them. If I did, I would be going back on my word and ignoring the rule. I simply said, "Well, I did have these chocolate chip cookies for you"—I paused and tasted one—"but since you asked, no one will get them." I walked across the hall and gave the cookies to Ms. Hopkins to share with her class. Not a single student in that class ever asked me about a reward again. It's a hard lesson to learn, but if it will help the kids to learn to appreciate their efforts over their rewards, it will have been worth it.

★ RULE 16

Homework will be turned in each day for each subject by every student with no exceptions.

As adults, we are used to deadlines, due dates, and the pressure of being on time. We have to pay bills by a certain date, turn in assignments, and complete tasks quickly and efficiently. When I talk to my students about their work and what is required of them, I approach it from the standpoint that the work is part of the students' job. I want them to learn to be on time and proficient at a young age.

One way that I do that is by expecting every student to have every piece of homework every day. This is a nearly impossible task, right? Well, not really. If managed correctly, you can have every child in the classroom completing all assignments and turning them in on time, but it takes some effort. There are three things I do to make it happen.

pleting each assignment correctly. (And I give quite a bit of homework, by the way.) All I have to do is dump a box of mix in a bowl, bake it, cut it into squares, and take it to school. I don't think that is a lot to ask when you are getting such wonderful results from the entire class. The record for days in a row stands at sixty-two. I was a baking fool that year. That was my first year in Harlem, and those kids went from 30 percent homework participation to 100 percent, and their end-of-grade test scores were through the roof. I know a great part of that was because of their diligence and consistency with the work they were completing at home.

Third, *I use peer pressure* · As you can probably imagine, the class was not too thrilled when a student would forget his or her homework and cause the class to have to go all the way back to "0 Days in a Row." In fact, I never had to reprimand the child who broke the streak. The weight of having broken the streak was usually enough to bear. Actually, the amount of pressure I would let the other kids apply depended on the individual student.

Take Jarron. When he broke the streak, he didn't seem to mind. That was just his attitude. He was very carefree and seemed unconcerned with ruining it for the entire class. Well, I let the class lay it on thick. I saw them glare at him, I watched them fuss at him at lunchtime, I saw them reminding him of what the homework assignment was . . . and

I said nothing. I knew he could take the heat, and eventually, it did get him back on track.

Take Alison. The comments from the rest of the class would only annoy her and, in fact, had a negative impact. She had the attitude that she wasn't going to do the homework just because everyone was bugging her to do it. Therefore, if she didn't complete her work, I told the class to leave her alone, because if they started bugging her, I knew there was no way she would do it. When she was left alone, there was a far greater chance of her doing her work.

Take Abdula, the best and most prepared student in the class. She cared what her classmates thought of her, and she would rather eat nails than disappoint me. She was the sweetest, hardest-working student . . . and she was the student who broke the streak of sixty-two days in a row. By the time I got to her desk to check to see if she had her work, her face was covered in tears. It had been a mistake, a mistake anyone could have made. Abdula was responsible for helping her other siblings get ready for school, and in the rush out of her home, she had left her worksheets on the table beside her bed. I knew instantly she didn't have the work, so I walked to the front of the room and I said, "Class, we need to have a talk. We all know that Abdula is one of the most dedicated and hardworking students in this class. She has given her all to make sure this class made it to the streak of sixty-two, and even though the streak will end today at sixty-two, I think we as a class need to give ourselves *and* Abdula a round of applause, because I am telling you right now, I bet there is no class *in this nation* that finished their homework sixty-two days in a row this year, and we have a lot to be proud of." Of course, no punishment went to Abdula; it wasn't necessary. How some situations are handled depends a lot on the child.

★ RULE 17

When we are in transition from one subject to the other, the change will be swift, quiet, and orderly. We should be consistently able to turn from one book to another, complete with all homework and necessary materials, as quickly as possible. The opportune amount of time to spend in transition should be less than ten seconds, and we will work toward a goal of seven seconds.

In our daily lives, we are faced with multiple tasks that we must accomplish each day. Often, instead of completing all of the tasks in an orderly fashion, we are interrupted by distractions such as the telephone, that tempting TV show, that comfy couch, or conversations with coworkers. We could be so much more efficient if we could just stick to our goals, complete them, and then use the remaining time for our leisure activities. I try very hard to get my students to stay on task, take care of business first, and remain motivated until the job at hand is complete.

In my first year of teaching, I noticed that when we would finish one subject and get ready to begin another, the students would start to talk, move around, hunt for homework, get up to sharpen pencils, and waste a great deal of time trying to get organized. I decided to make subject transitions like a game. I told the class that when they first come to class in the morning, they should organize all of their materials so that they would be within reach. Then, when we finished with one subject and I would say, "Okay, now let's get out our math books and homework," the kids could put away the materials we had been working with and get out the things needed for math in a matter of seconds. Sometimes it would get tricky, for example, when I had to use the overhead projector. This required closing the blinds, turning off the lights, closing the door, wheeling out the projector, plugging it in, and pulling down the screen in addition to the students getting out their materials. In order to accomplish this, I assigned each of the necessary tasks to one student. Then, when I said I needed to use the projector, everyone jumped into action and within a matter of seconds it was ready to go. Teachers who would observe my class always commented on how quickly the kids would have the entire room ready for the overhead. Sometimes I would be at the front of the room talking, and a kid might say she couldn't see what I drew on the board and I would say, "Okay, let me show you on the overhead." I would start to walk toward the middle of the room, and before I could get there, the projector had been wheeled there and plugged in, the blinds were closed, lights off, screen down, and pen handed to me. I would casually take the pen and begin to write on the overhead as if it were nothing out of the ordinary. When teachers would ask how in the world I got the kids to do it, I would tell them that it is easy; kids love to help, they get a kick out of trying to move from one task to another as quickly as possible, and we practiced it over and over again. Before the end of the first month, if you do it correctly, the class will be performing like clockwork.

★ RULE 18

You will make every effort to be as organized as possible.

I come across as possibly the most disorganized person in the world. My desk in my classroom is nothing more than a huge mound of papers, folders, books, napkins, and food— yes, food. At times, I will jar the desk by accident and it will lead to an avalanche of chaos that causes kids nearby to have to raise their feet. If you talk to any of my former students, I am sure they will tell you about week-old glasses of tea, half-eaten doughnuts, and other items that litter my desk; but I am sure they will also tell you that I know where everything on the desk is and that anything I want is within my grasp within a matter of seconds.

Keeping in mind my propensity for clutter, you may understand why I have a high tolerance for students who maintain cluttered desks. This tolerance comes with a warning, though. I tell the students that I have no issues with how the insides of their desks look. I do, however, have a problem if they are not able to quickly produce work, notebooks, or other items that I ask from them. I taught one student in Harlem, named Marvin, who rivaled me in terms of clutter, but he always managed to have whatever I asked of him right at the tips of his fingers. There was another kid in Harlem, Shomond, who couldn't find water if he were in the ocean. Each time I saw that his inability to find his materials was due to disorganization, I would pick up his entire desk and turn it upside down, watching all of his cluttered items fall to the floor. He would then be asked to find his homework and instructed not to place anything back into the desk that wasn't a necessity. This may be seen as harsh, but it is dramatic, it sticks in the kids' minds, and the times when kids can't find materials decreases drastically. It is not done in anger or to humiliate in any way; it is done to teach, and I make sure I explain that to the students.

Each year, I always ask my former students' new teachers how they are performing in class. Mainly, I am interested in seeing in which areas I had prepared the students well, as well as the areas where my students have weaknesses. This is sometimes hard to do and very humbling, because it isn't easy hearing a teacher tell you how your students went to her unprepared. If you are really interested in becoming a better teacher, though, I think it is a necessary evaluation, and besides, it is rewarding when you hear positive comments. For example, teachers in the past have said, "I can definitely tell which of my students you taught, because their writing skills are superior to the rest of the class." That is wonderful to hear, but one area where teachers always used to point out weakness in my students, more so than the other students in their classes, was organization. It killed me to hear that, because I thought it must have something to do with the way I was preparing them.

One summer, I was determined to do something that would help to make my students become more structured. First, I went shopping and bought a set of the materials I wanted each of my students to have. I found a big ol' binder that would hold their notebooks, loose-leaf paper, pens and pencils, calculator, and calendar. Then I purchased the small, hundred-page notebooks that I wanted them to have and other items, like crayons, a ruler, a stapler, etc. I also got a box of tissue, because I found that I would buy tissue all year, because the kids' noses were constantly running.

To keep from having to pay for it myself, I just added it to their supply list. The next thing I did was place the items out on my living room floor and take a picture of them. I then wrote a letter to the kids, explaining the supplies they would need for the year, and I attached the picture to it. They received this three weeks before school began, so the parents had plenty of time to find the necessary materials. This was such a good idea. In past years, before I sent out the supply list letter, students would walk in on the first day of school equipped with a lot of materials they did not need, and I hated it. The kids, and the parents too, were usually so excited about the school year that they would go ahead and get all of their supply shopping done, even though much of it was for naught. When my students' parents got the picture and letter, they were so appreciative. They weren't rushed to find the supplies, they knew exactly what I wanted them to buy, and they didn't waste any money buying items the kids really didn't need.

On the first day of school, almost all of the students had all the supplies. I have found that all parents, regardless of their income, are very supportive of the beginning-of-the-year need for school supplies. I was able to go through each item the class had purchased and describe when it was to be used and how they were supposed to label each assignment. I showed them how to keep their homework listed on their calendar pages and where to place papers that had been graded. After walking the class through the system, they became the most organized class I had ever taught, and it made my life a lot easier. When I needed the students to hand in their homework, they all knew where it was. If I needed the kids to get out their review sheets, they went to them immediately. Also, when I had parent-teacher conferences, I was able to go through each child's notebooks and binders with the parents and quickly find any materials, worksheets, or tests that I needed. The main thing I learned from that year is that my students enjoyed being organized, and they appreciated the system. After being shown how to be organized, they were able to use that skill not only during that school year but in future years and on into their professional careers.

I would recommend that if you are in a profession where you have to instruct others, be as specific as possible about what you expect. If you have to, take pictures and give them handouts detailing exactly what you want them to do or produce. Teach them how to be organized by showing them examples of how you yourself are organized and the type of structure you expect from them. One thing I have observed is that you should never assume anything about what a student, or any person, knows or understands how to do. It is always best to be specific about your expectations.

★ RULE 19

When I assign homework, there is to be no moaning or complaining. This will result in a doubled assignment.

Think about the place where you work. . . . Now think about the people you work with. How many of them would you say are positive people? How many are negative? Which would you rather spend time talking to and working with? I think the answer is obvious, but still, so many people carry negative attitudes and seem to complain about anything that they are asked to do or that demands them to put forth effort.

I hate being around people like that because it really annoys me to hear people complain about life. Sometimes there are things we just have to do that we may not want to do at that very moment, but it is our obligation and so we should do it anyway, without moaning or making comments about how we don't want to. Many times, more effort and energy is wasted avoiding something than it would have taken to complete the task. Sometimes when your kids ask you for help on their homework, or when an elderly relative wants you to visit or the lawn needs mowing, you just don't feel like doing it. That is natural, but it is still an obligation, and it is something that should be done without complaining or giving off a feeling of lethargy.

I try to instill a positive type of attitude in my classroom, and under no circumstances do I allow my students to whine or fuss about any assignments or expectations of them. The punishment I use for this rule, doubling assignments for moaning, however, has given me a lot of grief in the past. Teachers always say, "Mr. Clark, I really don't agree with that Rule 19; you should *never* use homework as a punishment." I understand their point of view, but at the same time, moaning and complaining about work that is assigned will not be tolerated. In order to keep it from happening, the consequences for it must be fairly drastic. What do you think is worse? Having a class moan about each assignment, spreading the negative feelings about doing the work, *or* having to double the assignment once or twice but having the kids accept each assignment thereafter with no moaning or complaints?

I tell my students that if they do feel the homework is too much for one night, they are welcome to voice their concerns. They must do it in a way, however, that is respectful and stated without whining or complaining. For example, I tell the kids they can state their feelings like this: "Mr. Clark, several of us in the class are performing in a show tonight at the community center. Do you think there is any way you could reduce the number of pages we need to read for homework?" I am always willing to work with kids on issues like that, and I always reduce the amount for the entire class, not for just the ones who have obligations that would keep them from completing all of the work.

★ RULE 20

While you are with a substitute teacher, you will obey the same rules that you follow when I am with you. (I know this is hard, but it is important.)

We all know what it is like when the boss is away from the office and the workers aren't necessarily in prime production mode. It's the old adage, "When the cat's away, the mice will play." I have seen it in my life when the Dunkin' Donuts manager was out of the store and we would play hide-and-seek, or when the principal was away from the school and some teachers would just hand out worksheets and call it a day. I want my students to have the mind-set that they are working for themselves and to have pride in their work, whether a boss is standing right over them or not. I want them to be the type of individuals who will give a job 110 percent because they want to and not because they have to.

Instilling that in twelve-year-olds can be challenging, because students can smell a substitute a mile away. They can sense an approaching illness that may cause their teacher to be absent days before any doctor would see it coming. And they can make life hell for the substitute who is new to them and demonstrates the least amount of fear.

I can remember what it was like to be in junior high. I remember the thrill when I saw that lenient substitute walk in the door. I remember once in seventh grade when, while a substitute was in the room, my fellow classmates and I launched an all-out war on one another. The girls were using rubber bands that Ginger Branch was providing from the supply that was meant to be used for her braces. The boys were picking red berries off Mrs. Gardener's plants that lined the wall next to the windows. There were rubber bands flying here, red berries flying there, and an oblivious substitute teacher sitting at the desk reading a Danielle Steel novel, unaware of what was going on outside of the pages of her book. When Mrs. Gardener walked in the next day, she looked at us, looked at her plants, and looked back at us and said, "What in the hell happened to my berry bushes?" It was not a pretty sight.

In order to keep my kids from performing as I once did, I use several techniques. The first one is that I talk to the kids a great deal about maintaining order in the classroom even when I am not there. I warn them to be on their best behavior, and I tell them that if I find out anyone was unruly, the consequences are going to be severe when I return. I love that phrase. "The consequences will be severe." It is great because I am not *really* saying what I am going to do, so I am not holding myself to anything. Chances are, the whole class could be bad, and I don't want to find myself with thirty-seven kids serving detention for a month. By saying only that it will be "severe," I could really just give them the lecture of their lives and act very disappointed in them and have kept my word. Anyway, when I return to school after that first absence, I make sure the substitute has left me clear notes about what occurred in the class. Then, if there is a child who misbehaved, and I can verify it, I have to make an example of that kid. It is unfortunate, but it is necessary. The entire class will be watching how I handle the situation, and if I do nothing, or if the consequences aren't serious, then the next day I am absent is going to be a field day for the kids. I am usually very vocal with the child in front of the class, and I will hand down a week's detention and let the child know I will be contacting the parents. I want that moment to stick in the kids' minds so that they will remember it the next time they are with a substitute.

I have to be honest with you, though. There have been times when the substitutes for my classes have been rude with the students, unreasonable, and not adept at handling a group of students. In those situations, I put almost as much blame on that person for the misbehavior of my students. I never let my students know that; I continue to act angry with them and like the world is coming to an end, but I forgo any consequences. I play the ol' game of "oh you have made me so upset and you are going to regret the consequences," but nothing really comes of it. This is one of my usual statements: "You know, kids, I am constantly giving everything I have for you. I work myself sick and continue to take you on trips, provide you with the best education possible, and this is the way you show me your appreciation. Well, I have to tell you, when you do things like this, it makes me not want to follow through with some very neat things I had planned for our class, and that is a shame." That speech works likes a charm.

My best technique for getting kids to behave for a substitute actually requires a lot of effort on my part, but it is extremely successful. When I know I am going to be absent, I take the school's video camera home with me and I record myself teaching the day's lessons. I will say something like, "Okay, students, now I need for you to get out your novels and turn to page 134. Mrs. Jenkins"—who is the substitute—"if you will please press pause and then press play when all of the students are on the correct page." I then read to the students, stopping to discuss points and clarify items that I think they would have questions about. The key to this, however, is a little trick I pull on the kids. First, I tell them at the beginning of the video that I can see each

and every one of them in the class, and that if they mis-
behave I will know it. Of course, this sounds ridiculous to
them, but the day before I'm out I always meet with a couple of students and swear them to secrecy. I tell one kid
that when I say I can see the kids in the class, I want him
to say, "Mr. Clark, can you really see us?" Then, when the
video is playing and the kid asks if I can see the class for
real, I reply, "Yes, Berry, I can see you! Now you better pay
attention!" It always freaks out the students, and I have even
shocked a few substitutes here and there.

There are several reasons I like doing the video. First,
the kids don't miss a day of instruction. I am "there" to
continue teaching the next day's lesson. Second, I don't have
to worry about writing up lesson plans for the substitute.
The plans consist of "Press play," then "Press stop." Third,
the kids appreciate the effort I take to make the video. They
don't always tell me, but when it comes up, I can tell it
meant a lot to them that I took the time to make a video
for them so that they wouldn't have to do mounds of worksheets and reading. Fourth, discipline is at a minimum. Substitutes comment on how easy it is to control a class when
all they have to do is sit back and take the names of kids
who aren't paying attention to the video, but they always say
that every kid watches the video and pays attention. I act
goofy and do neat stunts on the tape, so the kids get into it
and really enjoy watching.

This idea might also be useful when you are going to be away from your own children while you are on a business trip or on vacation. You can sit down in front of a camera and read one of their favorite storybooks to them. Then, when the child is missing you, he can play the video over and over as many times as he likes. We are now in the communications age, and just because you aren't there, it doesn't mean you can't be present.

RULE 21

We will follow certain classroom protocols. We will be organized, efficient, and on task. In order to do so, we will follow these rules:

A. *Do not get out of your seat without permission. Exception: If you are sick, leave immediately.*

B. *Do not speak unless:*

1. *You raise your hand, and I call on you.*
2. *I ask you a question and you are responding.*
3. *It is recess or lunch.*
4. *I instruct you otherwise (for example, during group work).*

this, I hope that you don't get the impression that my room is all structure and no fun, because actually I think the room is a very fun and exciting place to be. At times there is a lot of chaos and we are having a blast, but I know that if I need to get the kids back on task and organized, all I have to do is say the word and I will have complete silence.

The reason I don't allow my students to talk is because most classes have not been able to do so without getting out of hand. Perhaps it has been that the groups of kids I have worked with were high energy, or perhaps it is because of the number of kids in the classroom; in New York City I had thirty-seven kids in my classroom all day. Nevertheless, in order to get the groups focused and on task I have had to take away all speaking privileges unless we are in a class-room discussion, they have questions, or I call on them. Usually after a few months I will stop being so strict with the rule, and there will be whispers now and then, but it never gets out of hand. Once you have that type of control over a group, you can do some really neat projects. There have been times when we have done group projects and used glue, ribbons, balloons, and just about anything you can think of, but the kids remained focused and organized. I call it "organized chaos." We are able to do group work and have a lot of fun, but it is orderly and we get much more accomplished. If you don't have that structure in the classroom and you try to do hands-on cooperative learning, you are going to have a zoo.

⭐ RULE 22

You may bring a bottle of water and leave it on your desk. Do not ask me if you can get water while I am teaching a lesson. You can even have food at your desk as long as others don't see it and I don't hear you eat it.

We all perform better when we are comfortable with our surroundings. Think about where you work. Do you keep coffee or a drink near you? Is there candy nearby? Do you have snacks with you as you watch TV? It is natural and comforting to want to have some personal control over our immediate surroundings.

Throughout my entire life as a student, I had to have a handful of candy in my pocket to get me through the day. I can't even imagine how many times in grade school I was told to spit out my gum or throw away my candy. I can remember how excited I was when I got to college and discovered I could take a slice of pizza and a drink to class with me if I wanted to. I was in heaven. There was just something comforting about having that drink and food there by my side. Every time I would visit my mother at work, she would always have a Pepsi and dish of Hershey's Kisses on her desk. She told me she couldn't perform without them. It struck me as odd that in classrooms, any type of food, drink, or even gum was not allowed. This may be surprising to you coming from someone with such a strict classroom, but actually, students having drinks and food in the class doesn't bother me at all. When I was teaching in Harlem, there were days when it would be very hot in our classroom, and the kids were constantly asking if they could get water. It drove me crazy, but I couldn't argue with it. I decided that I would just allow them to keep a bottle of water on their desks, and that way, I would not have kids getting up and down to get water all through my lessons.

A few years ago, I even decided to allow the kids to have food if they wanted, but there were stipulations that went along with it. First, they must not make noise opening any packages. Second, no one in the class must be able to hear them chew. Third, they must not leave any crumbs or food remains around their desks. The kids were so excited and they loved having the items at their desks, and most of them abided by the rules really well, but there were some slight problems. . . . One girl, Tamanda, had more food in her desk than aisle 9 at the Piggly Wiggly. There would be half-eaten sandwiches, smashed potato chips, chocolate pudding, jelly beans, and anything else you can think of crammed in her desk among all of her books and papers. It was a hassle keeping that girl from making a mess, and finally I had to take her food privileges away.

Speaking of Tamanda's desk, it was always a source of conversation, and I have a whole list of stories about it. One day the science teacher, Mrs. Scofland, did a lesson that required the use of food coloring. When she was finished with the lesson, a small container of green food coloring was missing. I asked if anyone had it, but no one raised a hand. Later, I looked back to see that Tamanda's face was completely green! She had hidden the bottle in her desk, and apparently she had spilled it all over her hands. She wasn't aware of it, but she had rested her face in her hands and her face was completely covered! I decided to ask again . . . "Class, are you sure that *none* of you have the missing container of green food coloring?" No hands rose, so I went back to teaching. A few minutes later, I couldn't stand it any longer, and I said, "Tamanda, are you sure that *you* don't know where the food coloring is?" and she replied, "No sir," as if I were crazy to think she could have it. I simply replied, "Well, Tamanda, just in case you do have it in your desk, I somehow feel that you have already been punished enough." She eventually discovered it was all over her face and that I knew she had taken the container, but by that time, half the school had seen her green face and I felt that was sufficient punishment.

★RULE 23

Quickly learn the names of other teachers in the school and greet them by saying things like, "Good morning, Mrs. Graham," or "Good afternoon, Ms.

Ortiz. That is a very pretty dress." (Note: If you are in line with the rest of the class, you are not allowed to speak to the teachers at that time because the no-talking rule is in effect. You should speak to other teachers if you are entering or leaving school, on recess, on an errand, or changing classes.)

It always surprises me when I talk to people who don't know the names of their neighbors or who can't name all of their immediate coworkers. It is a shame that people don't go out of their way to introduce themselves more often, especially when there is someone new in the workplace or in the neighborhood/community. I hope that as my students go through life they will learn to get to know the people who live and work around them and try to make people who are just starting out at their job or where they live feel comfortable and welcomed in their new surroundings. I want them to get used to learning the names of those around them and to make an effort to be kind and polite to everyone. I think this makes for a more comfortable and enjoyable place to live and work, and they will be far happier in those environments.

Of all the schools I have visited around the country, I have seen more success and always felt more at home in smaller schools where all of the teachers know all of the students and vice versa. I have heard many teachers say they feel the key to creating a successful school environment is having smaller class sizes. I don't necessarily feel that is the case. I have visited some large schools of over 1,000 students where there is a lot of funding and each class contains fewer than twenty-two students. In those schools, however, the kids seem to slip through the cracks, and their own identity in the school is missing. At Snowden Elementary, there were times when we had classes of over thirty students, but we still maintained the "home" feeling in the school because we all knew one another and there was a strong element of trust in the building. I think the key might be not how many kids are in the classroom, but rather how positive and welcoming the atmosphere of the school makes the kids feel.

When I went to PS 83 in Harlem, I felt that trust and comfortable feeling was established to a point. The assistant principal, Mrs. Castillo, was an outstanding individual who acted as the mother figure of teachers and students alike. She knew the name of every child and was respected by all. There were also teachers who had been there for four or five years whom the students respected and loved. On the other hand, there were a number of new faces in the school each year. My first week at the school, there were over ten new teachers. Of the initial group, after a couple of weeks, five had left and five more were added. Of those new five, three left and were replaced by three new ones, all before

Christmas. This made it hard for bonds to be made that would unify the entire school. Therefore, to help matters, I asked the kids to learn the names of all of the teachers in the school to help create that unified atmosphere. I feel that if the kids know everyone in the school, they will feel more comfortable in the school. The more adults in the school they know, the more people there will be for them to turn to when they have problems or need help.

In addition, as a teacher, it is nice when the students know who you are and speak to you. Imagine a new teacher walking into a school for the first time. He or she is probably nervous about entering the new environment and worried the kids won't like him or her. In most schools, teachers have activities to welcome new faculty members, but I think it can be more effective if the students are giving a positive welcome as well.

RULE 24

Flush the toilet and wash your hands after using the rest room. When in a public rest room, get a paper towel before washing your hands. After washing your hands, use the paper towel to turn off the faucets and to press the dispenser to get another paper towel to dry your hands. (Or use the towel to press the button to start the dryer.) The last thing you want to do is touch areas with clean hands that others have touched with dirty hands.

This rule may be a bit extreme, and you may not see the need to use a paper towel to turn off the faucet. I can understand that. All I am really asking is that people take cleanliness into account when they're using a public rest room. We all know that bathroom facilities can sometimes make that a very hard thing to do. It drives me crazy when there is no soap in those little dispensers you have to pump, and just what is going on with those sensored faucets that only run water for about 1.5 seconds? I find myself waving my hands under the faucet to get it to begin, but by the time I get both hands under the water, it has shut off. It makes washing your hands more of a chore than it should be.

In addition to the difficulties with actually washing your hands, public rest rooms can be a nightmare. From unflushed toilets to floors littered with tissue, it can be a pretty unsanitary and disgusting experience.

My first year of teaching, I kept noticing how the urinals in the boys' rest room were never being flushed. It drove me crazy! I asked the kids why they never flushed the toilet and I got two responses: 1. I don't want to touch the handle because it's nasty. 2. We don't flush at home unless it is a number two because it wastes water and costs money.

To solve the first problem, I told the kids to get a paper

towel after they finished using the rest room and use the paper towel to touch the handle. For the second one, I explained to them that if their urine sits in the toilet, it will cause germs around that area and make others, including them, sick. I then asked how many of them liked to use a toilet that had someone else's urine in it. No one did, of course, and so I reinforced the need to take care of your own business and not to leave it there for others to deal with. Thankfully, the kids took what I said to heart and there were clean bowls from then on out. The kids in my class even started to grab other kids and remind them to flush if they were just going to walk away.

The second problem I saw with the bathroom is that kids take their dirty hands and turn on the faucet, then they wash their hands, and then they turn off the faucet where they had just placed their dirty hands. In order to solve that problem, I asked the kids to get a paper towel before washing their hands. I tell them to use that towel to turn off the faucet after washing their hands and to also use it to dispense another paper towel. (I know this may seem neurotic, but when you are a schoolteacher and you come in contact with every germ known to man, you learn that if you want to survive you have to stop the germs where they start!)

In terms of overall bathroom cleanliness, I talk to the students a lot about how hard the custodians work and how it is easy for us to help them by doing a few very small things. The first is making sure that there are no paper towels left on the bathroom floor. This is nearly impossible because teenage boys think they are Michael Jordan, and they're not. Missed baskets always line the floor around the trash can. I make a point to tell the boys, and the girls as well, to take a paper towel and go around the entire bathroom and pick up any trash left on the floor and dispose of it. I make sure to tell them that I don't care if they did it or not, but what matters is that the floor is clean when they leave. It has made a huge difference in the look of the room, and the kids take pride in that.

★ RULE 25

We will often have visitors to our school. If someone is coming to visit our class, I will send two students to the front door of the building. You will have a sign welcoming the person. When our visitor arrives, you will shake hands, tell him or her who you are, and welcome the person to our school. You will then take the visitor on a small tour of the building before bringing him or her to the classroom.

This technique can be used whether you are having visitors come to your office or you are having a guest at a party who doesn't know anyone other than you. It is all about making the person feel comfortable and welcomed in their new surroundings. For the visiting businessperson, have him greeted at the door and given a brief tour of your office. Have him taken personally to your office and introduced to you. For the party guest, have another friend of yours meet him at the door and take him around the party, introducing him to your other guests.

Entering an unknown environment can be intimidating and scary. When I was a sophomore in high school, my parents moved within North Carolina from Chocowinity to Belhaven, and I had to go to a new high school where I knew no one. On that first day I was terrified. My parents told me that the school would assign me a buddy to show me around on the first day, but that never happened. I was all alone, and going from class to class was bad enough, but I was most dreading lunchtime, because I knew I was going to be eating alone. Luckily, during fourth period I was as-signed a lab partner, Anita Cahoon. She turned to me and said, "You must be new, so you're going to eat lunch with me and my friends and I won't take no for an answer." She didn't have to worry about that; I was so relieved. I ended up becoming best friends with Anita and her friends, and I grew to love that school. I never forgot, however, the awk-ward feeling on the first day of not knowing anyone or where to go or what to expect.

Recently, I had to visit the Muzak corporate office in

Charlotte, and I was floored by their welcome. They had someone greet me at the door, take me on a tour of the facility, and introduce me to all of the workers. They had my favorite foods, sweet tea and fruit, prepared as a snack for me. Before I left, they gave me a Care basket that contained a T-shirt, a coffee mug, and several other souvenirs of the visit. They certainly rolled out the red carpet and made me feel welcome. Although I might not be able to go to those lengths for everyone who visits our classroom, I want to make sure everyone who visits feels welcome. Walking into a school can be especially intimidating when you don't know where to go or who you need to speak with. In order to manage this situation, I have two students wait at the front door with a welcome sign that has the visitor's name written clearly. This is carefully timed so that little instruction time is missed.

When the guest arrives, I have the students greet him or her and conduct a small tour of the school. They then escort the person to the room and introduce him or her to the class. This process takes a lot of practice, and I usually have a group of kids stay after school one day to practice giving the tour. We go over introductions, information they should give, and questions they should ask. This is a respectful gesture that is appreciated by everyone who visits the school.

★ RULE 26

Do not save seats in the lunchroom. If someone wants to sit down, let him or her. Do not try to exclude anyone. We are a family, and we must treat one another with respect and kindness.

We have all felt left out at some time or another, often at the mercy of other adults. When kids in the classroom are the ones being excluded, it can be a nightmare for any teacher. I hate to see kids who are isolated and left alone. I start from day one talking to the students about being a family and including one another. I tell them to be a friend to everyone in the class and not just a select few. I also tell them, however, that they don't have to like everyone in the class. I tell them that, as an adult, I don't like every adult I meet. I tell them that it is only human not to like everyone, but that I make sure to try to treat each person with kindness and respect regardless of my feelings. I inform them that I expect the same type of behavior from them as well.

If I notice at lunchtime that kids are sitting in the same seats every day or that seats are being saved, I give the kids a warning. If it happens again, I utilize a seating chart. I make sure to seat students in a way so that everyone has someone to talk to and no one will be left out. I usually tell them they will have to sit like that until I say otherwise. (I love that phrase . . . "until I say otherwise." It is often not a good idea to put an amount of time on a punishment, because you never know what may happen to cause you to want to lessen it or lengthen it.)

It takes a while for students to learn to accept everyone, because there is a certain amount of safety in being part of a clique. Even as adults, we want to have a sense of belonging, and unfortunately the bonding of some will mean the exclusion of others. It's okay to have groups of friends, but I try to teach my students that it is important to make sure they and their friends accept others and try to include others in their activities.

★ RULE 27

If I or any other teacher in the school is speaking to or disciplining a student, do not look at that student. You wouldn't want others looking at you if you were in trouble or being reprimanded, so don't look at others in that situation. If you are the student I am talking to, do not get angry or fuss at students who are looking at you. Let me know and I will handle the situation.

Julia Jones is the sole origin of this rule. Julia was in trouble on a consistent basis. You name it, she did it. Whenever I would try to reprimand her, matters would only escalate when other students watched as she was scolded. She would lash out at them, verbally or physically, and become extremely hostile. I knew I had to keep that from happening at all costs, so I told all of the students that if I am disciplining another student, they are not to look. They are to keep their heads down or facing forward. This rule worked like a charm, not only with Julia, but with all of the students. Imagine being pulled over for speeding. The cop asks you to get out of the car. As you are talking to him, every passerby turns to stare at you. It's not a good feeling, and in fact, it makes matters worse. My co-teacher from North Carolina, Barbara Jones, always said her greatest fear was that she was going to be pulled over by a cop and that every school bus was going to pass by with all of her students waving and pointing out the windows. It is one thing to be punished, and another to be in trouble and have everyone know about it and watch as you are scolded. In school, kids are inevitably going to get in trouble and there will be times when they must be reprimanded. In order to avoid the embarrassment and the anger that being a public spectacle can create, I make sure the kids know and understand this rule. I also make sure the kids understand that if a student stares at someone I am talking sternly to, the student who is staring will be punished as well.

★RULE 28

If you have a question about your homework, you may call me. If I am not there to answer the phone, please leave a message in the following manner: "Hi, Mr. Clark, this is _____. I need help with the _____ homework. You can call me back until ____:00. Thank you." There is no need to leave this message fourteen times.

In today's world, it is crucial that businesses be accessible to their clients at all times. People feel more comfortable when they can contact the people who are providing them services at any time they have questions or need to talk about business. In order to be successful, you have got to be accessible, and I take that attitude into my classroom as well. I have no problem whatsoever giving the students my number, although many teachers do not give out their home numbers, and I can't blame them. It could turn into a nightmare if your phone is constantly ringing. However, it really isn't that bad, because most students will not call, but I think it makes them feel good to know that they can call me if they need to. It gives them a type of security, and it shows them that I care enough about them to share my personal home time with them if they need me. I do spend time explaining to the students what is an appropriate call.

I tell them that calling me to find out what their homework is isn't acceptable. They should have made sure to copy it down in class, and if they didn't copy it down, they need to call a fellow student. If they call me, I will tell them the assignment, but they will have silent lunch and lose their recess on the next school day. A call that would be appropriate is a call about problems with the homework. Oftentimes in a class of over thirty students, it is hard to give individual attention to the ones who need it. Also, many kids are embarrassed to admit in front of other students that they need help. Giving my phone number to them gives those kids an opportunity to get individual attention from me that isn't possible in school. In Harlem, there was a girl named Maria who was very quiet and shy in the classroom. She never raised her hand or let on that she was confused. Each night, however, she would call me on the phone and we would speak for about five minutes about the night's assignment. She would often just need more clarification and a little help getting started. For Maria, that made all the difference in her school year, and not only academically. She knew she wasn't alone and that she had me to support her and help her when she needed me.

For teachers who are worried their phones may ring off the hook, I rarely had more than one call a day. It was important to give my number, though, because no child could walk in my class and claim they didn't do their homework because they didn't understand it. I take away that excuse, because they could have called me.

★ RULE 29

There are several manners dealing with food that you must follow: I call these my ABC's of Etiquette.

A. *When you first sit down for a meal, immediately place your napkin in your lap. If your silverware is wrapped in a napkin, unwrap it as soon as you sit down and place the napkin in your lap.*

B. *When you are finished eating, place your napkin on the table to the left of your plate. Place it loosely beside the plate. Don't crumple it, because you don't want to seem untidy. Don't fold it too neatly, because you don't want the restaurant to think you assume they are going to use it again. Never leave your napkin on your chair. This implies that the napkin is too dirty to be left on the table. Also, in some cultures, leaving the napkin on the chair is known as a way to say that you don't intend to return to the restaurant again.*

C. *Never place your elbows on the table.*

D. *Use one hand to eat, unless you are cutting or buttering food. Never have your fork in one hand and a glass in the other.*

E. *Do not lick your fingers. There is a napkin provided for the purpose of cleaning your fingers. There is no need to lick yourself clean.*

F. *Do not smack your lips and chew noisily.*

G. *Do not chew with your mouth open.*

H. *Do not talk with your mouth full. Sometimes people will place a hand over their mouth and talk anyway. Don't do that. Wait until you have swallowed your food to speak.*

I. *If something is caught in your teeth, don't go in after it; wait until you are in the rest room to remove it.*

J. *Do not slurp.*

K. *Do not play with your food.*

L. *If you drop your fork, napkin, or anything else on the floor, do not pick it up. It is very rude and unsanitary to place something on the table that has been on the floor. If you pick up something that has dropped and hand it to a waiter, then you will need to excuse yourself and wash your hands before continuing with your meal. The best way to handle a situation when something has dropped on the floor is to ask a waiter for a replacement; leave the old one on the floor.*

M. *You are to use your utensils for eating almost everything. Here are ten types of foods you may use your hands to eat:*

1. *Pizza*
2. *Bacon*
3. *Cookies*
4. *Bread (Always tear off a bite-sized piece to eat. If you are going to use butter, never butter the whole piece of bread; butter the piece you tore off, and eat that before tearing another piece.)*
5. *Corn on the cob (It is appropriate to eat across instead of eating around.)*
6. *Hot dogs, hamburgers, and sandwiches (including breakfast biscuits)*
7. *French fries and chips*
8. *Fried chicken*

9. Asparagus (yes, asparagus)
10. Small fruits (like grapes on a stem), apples, oranges, carrots, etc.

N. Never reach over someone's plate to get something. You should say, "Will you please pass the salt?"

O. Never start eating off of your tray until you are at your seat.

P. When we are eating at a restaurant, you are not to begin eating until everyone at the table has received their food.

Q. You should never complain if the line is too long, the food isn't good, or if there is a wait. You don't want to be negative to the point where you spoil the enjoyment of the event for others.

R. If you are unsure which silverware to use, simply start with the fork, knife, or spoon that is the farthest from your plate. On the left, you will have your salad fork on the outside and your dinner fork on the inside. On the far right, you will have your soupspoon. Beside it you will have the spoon you will use to stir your

coffee or tea, then your salad knife, and then
your dinner knife. The utensils above your
plate are to be used for dessert.

S. When you are finished eating, do not push
your plate away from you. Leave it where it
is in the setting. If you want to show you
have finished eating, you should lay your fork
and knife together diagonally across the
plate. You should place the fork with the
tines down, and you should have the sharp
side of the knife facing you. Of the two utensils, the fork should be closest to you.

T. Never place a piece of silverware that you
have used back on the table. Leave it on a
plate or saucer.

U. If you didn't use a utensil, do not place it on
a plate or saucer when you are finished. Just
leave it where it is.

V. Always look a waiter in the eyes when you
are ordering, asking a question, or saying
thank you.

W. Make a point to remember the waiter's name
when he introduces himself to you. Use his

name as often as possible throughout the course of the meal.

X. If you have to go to the rest room, you should stand up and say, "Excuse me," as you leave the table.

Y. When you are offered desserts or asked a question such as "What sides would you like?" or "What dressing would you like for your salad?" it is best to ask, "What are my options?" That way, you aren't going through a process of naming things the restaurant might not have.

Z. Never talk to waiters or waitresses as if they are servants. Treat them with respect and kindness, and remember, they are the ones who are fixing your food and bringing it to you. You do not want to be on the bad side of a waiter.

I realize expecting kids to abide by these rules may seem a bit much, but actually I have found that the kids really enjoy learning the manners and putting them into practice. It is always a shock to people when they walk into the lunchroom and see my kids eating with their napkins in their laps, eating with one hand, and using perfect table manners. In "Cafeteria World" that is almost an anomaly.

I remember the time when I was in junior high that my family and I were at my cousin Shelia's wedding. While we were at the very fancy reception dinner, everyone at the tables just sat quietly in front of the elaborate place settings, not knowing one another and struggling to make conversation. In the center of the table was a dish containing little pieces of butter in the shape of flowers. After about two minutes where no one at the table said a word, my mother, bless her heart, in an attempt to ease the tension, reached for one of the pieces of butter, saying, "Look, Ron, would you like a mint?" As she picked up the flower, it smashed between her fingers. She then realized it was indeed not a mint, and in her embarrassment she turned three shades of red, then started to laugh at herself. Soon the entire table was laughing and we ended up having a wonderful night of conversation and laughter.

Even though that situation turned out well, I don't want my students to end up in a position like my mother or me, feeling uncomfortable, not knowing what to do or how to handle themselves. Even if the kids never need to eat at a formal dinner, at least they will be prepared to, and if they have an opportunity to do so, there would be no reason for them to feel they aren't prepared to go or that they would be embarrassed.

★RULE 30

After we eat, we will clean up after ourselves. This includes cleaning off the tables and making sure we haven't left any trash on the floor or around the eating area. It is important to be responsible for your trash no matter where you are and to be sure not to litter.

As a general rule, kids are messy eaters. Visit a lunchroom, and you will most likely see napkins littering the floor, remains of spilled food, and lunch tables that are askew. That really bothers me, because if kids are allowed to get away with that in school, then they are going to carry that behavior with them when they are at McDonald's or any other restaurant or eating establishment. I make sure that when my students leave their tables, we leave them exactly as we found them. We pick up all of the trash, wipe the tables clean, and make sure there is no stray paper around the trash cans. In the beginning I have to remind them every day, but after I work with them for a couple of months, they know to pick up their trash before they leave. By the end of the year, there isn't any trash on the floor to pick up, because they have learned that instead of having to clean up after themselves, they can be more careful as they eat and there will be no mess to worry about.

I have always been annoyed by littering of any kind, not only in food establishments. I stress to the kids that they should take pride in their school and community, and not only refrain from littering, but they should also pick up trash that has been left by others. I often do small tests with kids to see if they are adhering to that rule. I will place a few pieces of trash around the room before the students arrive, and then I will see who picks them up. After everyone is seated, I will tell them that the ones who picked up the trash will get free ice cream at lunch. I always point out the kids who glanced at the trash but walked past it without picking it up. Believe me when I tell you that there will not be a piece of trash left on that floor for weeks after a trick like that.

One day I was reminding the students about not littering, and one boy named Pablo said, "Mr. Clark, the other day I was hanging out at the convenience store with my friends and we saw a sign they have up in there that says 'no littering,' so they must be serious about keeping trash off the floor too." I thought it was interesting that there was a sign inside the store that said no littering, so the next time I was there I looked for it. Sure enough, there was a sign, but it actually read, "No loitering." I thought of Pablo standing there with his friends, hanging out, making sure not to litter, but all the while they were doing the opposite of what the sign was asking.

The point, though, is that kids become aware of the importance of keeping areas clean and taking ownership of their own trash. I am always so proud of my students by the end of the year and the way they become conscious of their own actions and gain respect for their school and community and make sincere efforts to keep them clean.

RULE 31

When we stay in a hotel room, it is appropriate to leave a tip on the pillow for the hotel workers who are responsible for cleaning the room after our stay. Two to three dollars per night is an appropriate amount, depending on the cost of the room.

I have found that most students know they are supposed to tip a waiter or taxi driver, but most haven't heard they are supposed to tip in their hotel room as well. I recently was on a trip with some friends of mine, and one of my friends, Lloyd, left $12 on the dresser before he left the room. I asked him why he was leaving such a large tip, and he told me that his mother works in a hotel and that she always complains that most people don't leave any tip and that many just leave the change out of their pockets. Lloyd said he always tips extra to make up for the many rooms where there would be no tip at all. That just emphasized to me the importance of leaving some amount to show appreciation for having the room cleaned. I hope that by enforcing that gesture in my students now, it will have an impact on them and remain a practice they continue for the rest of their lives. When we are on trips, I don't expect the students to leave their own spending money as a tip. For all of our trips, we have had fund-raisers in order to pay for the entire trip, and the tip money is included as part of the budget.

I know that some people may not be accustomed to leaving tips in hotel rooms, because essentially they are leaving money for someone they will never see or have any contact with. Doing things for someone who can never thank you personally is the message of the saying "what goes around, comes around." You should be kind to everyone and show appreciation to those who do things for you, and in return it can bring only good things for you. Speaking of leaving tips, I think no one can appreciate how important it is to leave an appropriate tip unless you have worked for tips yourself. For example, I guarantee you that if you are waiting tables you will not find a better tipper than someone who has also waited tables.

RULE 32

When we ride on a bus, we will always sit facing forward. We will never turn around to talk to other

*students, stick anything out of the windows, or get
out of our seats. When we exit the bus, we will always thank the bus driver and tell him to have a
good day.*

This rule probably wouldn't be that important to me if I
didn't have to drive students on trips myself. It can be nerve-
racking! It is hard enough to drive a large vehicle, but then
you have the added pressure of having the lives of so many
students in your hands. The last thing you need is thirty
screaming kids to distract you and make driving even harder.

I have seen and heard nightmare stories about kids who
throw things out of bus windows and break other vehicles'
windshields. I have heard of students who were fighting on
the bus but the driver was too scared to get involved so he
didn't even bother stopping. There are times when objects
are actually thrown at drivers, and kids who try to make
them swerve and drive off the road. I know of one teacher's
daughter who was dared to moon a car out of the back
window of the bus; she did, and the driver of that car turned
out to be the superintendent. Oh me!

The school bus can be a place of chaos, and what worries me is that all of those chaotic actions lead to distractions
for the driver. I wouldn't want my child placed in a situation
like that. I make every attempt to stress to my students the
importance of sitting quietly, doing homework, or talking in

whispers to a friend. I tell them to avoid getting the attention of other students, standing up, turning around, or doing anything that would cause a large distraction.

I also tell my students that the kind of behavior I expect on a bus is the same as what I expect in a taxi, an airplane, or any other type of transportation. Out of consideration for the driver and the other passengers, it is always respectful to make as little noise as possible and not to cause any amount of commotion. In all cases, it is appropriate to thank the drivers and to wish them a good day.

★ RULE 33

When we go on field trips, we will meet different people. When I introduce you to the people, make sure that you remember their names. Then, when we are leaving, make sure to shake their hands and thank them, mentioning their names as you do so.

The first year my class was invited to the White House, the President and Mrs. Clinton took the time to shake the hands of each student and parent who was on the trip. I noticed that Mrs. Clinton was doing a very good job of remembering each student's name, and as we were leaving and she was telling the students good-bye, she was calling each child by name. I was really impressed by that, but it didn't end there. Two years later I was at the White House with a different group of students, and again we talked to Mrs. Clinton. Not only did she once again do a great job remembering each child's name quickly, she also asked me how some of my former students were doing, and she was asking about them by name. Now, I am sure part of this is due to the fact that Mrs. Clinton has an incredible memory, but I also noticed something that she does. When she is introduced to someone, she always replies to them and ends her statement by saying their name. This reinforces in her memory the name of the person and helps her to remember it. I started to teach my kids to do the same thing, and we practiced like this:

Mr. Clark: "Students, I would like to introduce you to Mr. Wallace, the owner of this theater."

Student: "It is a pleasure to meet you, Mr. Wallace. Thank you so much for giving us this tour of your theater."

Then, upon leaving . . .

Student: "Again, Mr. Wallace, on behalf of my fellow students I would like to thank you for the hospitality that you have shown us today. We have all learned a great deal about how thea-

We were at a pizzeria, and students were coming back to the table with five or six pieces of pizza on their plates. Since then I have set limits on how much the students can place on their plates. I tell them that they cannot cover more than three-quarters of the plate and that they cannot pile anything on top of something else. When kids are hungry, though, this rule can be hard to enforce.

When we were at Disney's American Teacher Awards and I walked to the podium to give my acceptance speech, I took four of my students onstage with me. I was thrilled to win for many reasons, and one of them is quite funny. I was excited that I won because I have always wondered where the winners go on award shows when they walk offstage. I used to wonder, "Who is back there, and just what are they doing?" Well, when the kids and I got to go backstage, I was glad to finally find out. There were reporters on one side for interviews, a large-screen TV showing what was going on with the show, and a replica of the onstage podium where we stood to have our pictures taken. There was also a buffet, and my students were allowed to fix small plates as I was interviewed. Suddenly, a lady came up to me and said that we had to make it back to our table quickly because the next award was about to be presented. As I called the kids over and told them we had to hurry back, I was stunned to see that one of my students, Sabrina, had piled nine hot wings on her plate. I said, "Sabrina, I can't believe you! Don't you remember that Rule 34 is about gluttony!" She replied that she was hungry, but I told her we didn't have time to eat because we had to hurry back to our table, and I told her to dump the plate in the trash. She did so, and we began to make our way back to our seats. As we meandered our way through table after table, passing guests such as Oprah Winfrey and Michael Eisner, I smiled and nodded my head in greeting. I glanced back to see three of my students, Brad, David, and Trevor, following me and doing the same very gracefully, but then I noticed Sabrina pulling up the rear, smiling at first, but then trying to discreetly take a bite of one of the chicken wings she was still holding!

Even though the enforcement of Rule 34 doesn't always work that well, kids usually get the idea and do really well with not being gluttonous. Sometimes when I pass out Rice Krispies treats or brownies to the students, there will be individuals who will glance over them, trying to find the biggest one for themselves. If I notice students doing that, I skip them and wait until everyone else has selected theirs before giving them a chance. The same applies when we have pizza parties; there will always be kids looking for the biggest slice of pizza, and it just takes constant reinforcement to remind the kids that they aren't the only ones who are hungry and who want the big piece of pizza. It takes a while to teach them to sacrifice their desire for the biggest piece in order to be respectful to others and not to assume that they deserve to have the biggest amount. After explaining why it's more polite to take a small amount, I always reward the students who try to put this into practice. For example, if I see a kid purposely take the smallest piece of pizza or brownie, I will go back to them after everyone else has gotten one and offer them an extra piece because their first one was so small. That reinforcement works well, and after a while the majority of the class will begin to put others before themselves.

★ RULE 35

Whether we are in school or on a field trip, if some-one drops something, pick it up and hand it back to them. Even if they are closer to the object, it is only polite to make the gesture of bending down to re-trieve the item.

Recently, I was walking out of Blockbuster, and my bank card and license fell out of my pocket. Before I could bend down, a little boy who was about ten feet away from me ran over and hurriedly picked up the cards and handed them back to me. I was so surprised and pleased. I thanked him loudly and looked around for his mother. She was watching him the entire time. She definitely looked like a lady who had her act together, and I am sure his good manners came from her instruction and guidance. Unfortunately, many parents don't see the need to teach such skills, and, therefore, our students end up oblivious to such basic acts of kindness.

In the classroom, it used to drive me crazy when a student's pencil would roll off of a desk and no one would pick it up. The kid would have to get up and walk around to get the pencil. Everyone else would just ignore it. After pointing out to kids how I expected them to pick up anything someone else dropped, they did it, and didn't have a problem with it. After a while, it really became commonplace to them. Once, we were on a field trip to see a play in Times Square and a lady who was finished with her pack of cigarettes just threw it on the ground. One of the little girls in the class, Jocelyn, ran and picked it up and chased down the woman saying, "Ma'am, you dropped this!" The woman looked at Jocelyn like she was crazy and put the empty pack back in her pocket. Well, picking up someone else's trash isn't exactly what I intended, but hey, I think it sent an important message to that lady nonetheless.

★ RULE 36

If you approach a door and someone is following you, hold the door. If the door opens by pulling, pull it open, stand to the side, and allow the other person to pass through first, then you can walk through. If the door opens by pushing, hold the door after you pass through.

After a few weeks of seeing kids try to cram through doors in the school and watching them enter restaurants as the door slammed on other customers, I knew I had to address this issue with my students. Teaching them small acts of kindness, such as letting someone else go through a door first as they hold it open, may seem insignificant, but it can go a long way toward helping students realize how to respect and appreciate others. If we don't point out these things to kids, most of them aren't going to figure them out on their own. Even with such a simple and basic rule as holding the door for others, I am always shocked at how many questions my students will have about it. They are always interested in hearing when it is appropriate to hold the door, how long they should stand there, if they should say anything, and where they should stand as they hold the door. They are anxious to learn exactly what they are supposed to do. I have found that is the case for almost all of these rules; the kids want to know just what is expected of them and how to show respect. Once they've been told, they're halfway there.

★ RULE 37

If someone bumps into you, even if it was not your fault, say, "Excuse me."

Often in school, a gentle bump can lead to World War III. It is all about heading that situation off before it happens. When I first told some of my students this rule, I didn't know how it would work, but after a month of practice and reminding them, I had huge boys, bigger than me, saying "Excuse me" right and left.

When my students from Harlem flew to Los Angeles to attend the American Teacher Awards, I was already there waiting for them. They were escorted by Mrs. Castillo, the assistant principal, and a group of teachers and parents. We had practiced airplane etiquette in my room the week before. I had turned the seats into aisles and taken on the role of a flight attendant who went down the rows taking orders and checking on the students. I wanted so badly for them to behave, but without my guidance, I was worried. At the airport, the first passengers off the plane looked around and said, *"Where is this Mr. Clark!?"* I thought, "Oh my Lord, what have these kids done?" Each person who got off the plane wanted to shake my hand. They said that when they saw the kids get on the plane they were thinking it was going to be a nightmare flight, but the kids were so polite and well mannered and respectful during the entire time. The captain of the plane had even made an announcement during the flight about the class and how well behaved they were. With air travel so difficult for everyone these days, the more pleasant we all can be, the better.

The most important compliment to me came from a lady

who said, "I just want you to know, over half of your students bumped into my arm as they were passing my seat in first class, but each and every one of them turned to say excuse me."

⭐ RULE 38

When we are on a field trip, there will be no talking as we enter a building. We will enter the building so quietly that no one will even notice that we are there. This rule applies to entering any place where people are gathered, whether it be the movies, a church, a theater, or any other venue.

I am sure that most teachers try to get their classes to be quiet when entering buildings and other areas while on field trips, but it is a lot easier to tell them what you expect from them before you are on the trip than to wait until you have arrived at your destination. My students also know that before we get on a subway, enter a restaurant, or go into any establishment, we are going to creep in there like mice. Over the years, we have certainly gotten some shocked, impressed, and appreciative looks. Most people, when they see a huge group of kids entering their building, think, *"Run for cover,"* but we often take people by surprise by getting all the way into a building before they even realize we are there.

In New York City, I took my class to see a play near Times Square. When we arrived at the theater we were a little late, and there were about twenty other classes lined up outside waiting to get in. The students from the other schools were not behaving and there was pandemonium. I told my students to stay in a line and maintain order. I told them that we would not carry ourselves like those other classes. Soon we started to file into the theater, and it was very disorganized. There was a lady trying to organize the groups and get them to their seats, but students were everywhere and no one really knew where to go. My class, observing our rule, walked in without a sound in two single-file lines. We stood near the door behind everyone else, and we waited. All of a sudden, the lady who was in charge noticed us, and she walked in our direction. She asked where the teacher was for our group, and I raised my hand. She said, "Very, very nice to meet you. Come this way." We were led into the theater, first, and we were given front-row seats.

Sometimes respect for others may not seem like it is going to have an impact, especially when you see no one around who is taking manners into consideration. However, that is usually the time when such kind actions will be most appreciated and recognized by others.

★ RULE 39

If we are on a field trip, it is a good idea to compliment something about the place where we are visiting. For example, if we visit someone's home, it would be a nice gesture to tell them that you think they have nice curtains. People are always self-conscious when they have guests visit their home, so you want to make them feel at ease. Also, if we are visiting other places, such as a museum or theater, it would be nice to comment on how beautiful the architecture is or to tell the guide that you think the facility is very nice.

When I visit the homes of my students' parents, I always try to put them at ease and make them feel as comfortable as possible. It is usually obvious that they have spent time cleaning and preparing for the visit, and I want them to know I appreciate their efforts and that I like their home. When I walk in, I find something I like or find interesting and I let the family know it. It helps to make them feel more comfortable and relaxed.

I rarely take the kids on field trips where they have to visit anyone's home, but we have on occasion, and I have asked them to remember this rule and to compliment the home when appropriate. On one trip, we were actually visiting a very important home, the White House. Three of my students, Brian, Ashley, and Kyeatta, were about to be introduced to the President. As we were waiting to enter the Oval Office, the students were talking with some of the President's aides. Brian said to one of them, "This is a lovely home, and that painting of that battle from the Revolutionary War is magnificent." The aides were equally shocked by Brian's manners as by his knowledge of the paintings throughout the house. The three students, who had to memorize all of the artwork in the White House before making the trip, ended up taking the aides on a bit of a tour, showing them all they had learned and pointing out interesting facts about the White House.

When we go on field trips like that, I always make sure that the students are prepared, know what they are going to see, and are given examples of things to compliment. Some may say I am putting words in their mouths, but actually, they are kids, I am their teacher, and they need practice. It is all about giving them tools that they will be able to use after they leave my classroom and are no longer under my guidance.

RULE 40

During an assembly, do not speak and do not look around and try to get the attention of your

friends in other classes. We must uphold an image
that shows we have our act together!

As a student, I can remember loving assemblies. As a teacher, I hate them. They disrupt the day, get the students off track, and provide many opportunities for misbehavior. Actually, those are the same reasons why I loved assemblies as a student.

In order to make the process more bearable, I explain to the students, in detail, exactly how I expect them to act when we are in the auditorium. On the first day of school when we come to this rule, I have the students line up, and we walk to the auditorium. I have them file into our designated rows, and I have them sit facing forward with their hands in their laps. No one is to put their arms on the armrests. I then go and sit at different places in the auditorium, calling individual students' names, throwing paper at them, and doing whatever I can to get their attention. My students practice staying focused, facing forward, and not talking.

On days when we have assemblies, I remind them of our practice session, and the kids remember exactly what I expect from them. They are always on their best behavior, even in the midst of the often chaotic auditorium.

★ RULE 41

When you answer the phone at your house, you must do so in an appropriate manner.

Kids, unless they are taught otherwise, have the worst phone manners imaginable. I can't tell you how many times I have called my students' homes and heard them answer the phone by saying, "Uh-huh?" or "Yeah?" When I ask for their parents, the usual response is, "Who's this?" When I say who I am, they become very quiet, but then they yell at the top of their lungs, "Ma! The teacher is on the phone for you!"

I make sure to tell my kids the appropriate way to answer the telephone. I tell them to use the following steps:

First: Say, "Hello" or "Hello, this is the Clark residence."

Second: The caller will ask if someone is there, and you should say, "Yes she is, may I ask who's calling?"

Third: Tell the person, "Hold on, please, and I'll get her."

Fourth: Place the phone on mute or cover the receiver with your hand and tell the person who is on the phone for her.

If the person is not home, I tell the kids to make sure they have pen and paper by the phone. The conversation should go like this:

First: Say, "Hello" or "Hello, this is the Clark residence."

Second: The caller will ask if someone is there, and you should say, "No I'm sorry, she's not. Would you like to leave a message?"

Third: If the caller doesn't want to leave a message, you can say, "Okay, she should be back in a couple of hours. Maybe you should try back then."

If the caller does want to leave a message, say, "Okay, can I get your name and number?" Make sure you repeat the number to the person so they will know you really copied it down and to make sure you have it copied correctly. When you are finished say, "I will make sure she gets this as soon as she gets in. Good-bye."

People form impressions when they call your home. From the first thing they hear on the other end of the line, they draw a mental picture of what the house looks like and what is going on in the environment. The last thing we want when we get a call, whether it is from a coworker, a bill collector, a friend, or whomever, is for the caller to get a negative impression about us, our families, and our home.

⭐ RULE 42

When we return from a trip, you will shake my hand as well as the hands of every chaperone. You will thank us for taking the time to take you on the trip, and you will let us know that you appreciate having the opportunity to go. I am not concerned with being thanked; I am concerned with teaching you that it is appropriate to show appreciation when someone has gone out of his or her way to help you.

I remember that when I was growing up my parents would always remind me to thank my teachers, Scout leaders, or other adults for anything they had done to help me. If I stayed over at a friend's house, I had to thank the parents for allowing me to stay and for cooking dinner or any other thing they did for me. I was always told to thank teachers after field trips or after any special effort they made to help me. This soon became second nature to me.

It amazed me when I started teaching that most of my students had not been taught those same types of manners. Sometimes it was awkward to ask the students to thank me for things I was doing for them, but I had to in order to get them into the hang of doing it. Even after much practice, there were still students who would forget to thank me and the other chaperones. It takes a lot of reinforcement before kids get the hang of it. There was one student in Harlem named Tyrone who was an exception. He wasn't one of the best students in the class in terms of behavior or academics, but every time I took students on trips throughout the city, I made sure he was included. I did so because after each trip, he was always genuinely grateful to have been invited, and he would make sure to shake my hand, look me straight in the face, and tell me that he had had a great time and appreciated my time and effort. He never forgot to thank me, and so I never forgot to include him.

★ RULE 43

When we are on field trips and we have to go up escalators, we will stand to the right. That will give other individuals who are in a hurry the option of walking up the left-hand side of the escalator. When we are going to enter an elevator, the subway, or a doorway, we will wait for others to exit before we enter.

After college when I moved to London, I was shocked at how polite everyone was in the subways. I was even more impressed when I traveled to Japan. In both places, people made extra effort to make way for others and respect others' space. On escalators, everyone stood to the right and walked to the left. On elevators, everyone would stand over to the side and allow individuals to exit before they would begin to enter. It was all very organized and the system was understood. In Japan, before the doors would open to the subways, everyone would get in a single-file line and enter the train without any shoving or pushing. Can you imagine trying to explain to subway riders at Grand Central Station that they are going to have to get in a line and enter the subway one by one?

As I have traveled around the United States this year, I have been frustrated at times with the lack of respect in public places. One thing that gets to me more than other things is that most people don't seem to know that on the escalators they need to "stand right, walk left." I am usually late to catch a plane or get to a meeting, and whenever I go to walk up the escalator, there will be just as many people standing to the left as there are to the right. Sometimes I just want to yell out, *"Stand to the right, walk to the left!"* I do suppress that urge, thank goodness, and instead I make sure to explain to my students how the system works, in hopes that they will help to enforce it and understand the importance of respecting others' space.

★ RULE 44

When in a line, walk single file, two to three feet behind the person in front of you with your arms at your sides. You should face forward at all times. There will be absolutely no talking.

The first day I started teaching in North Carolina, I knew the other teachers and the principal were curious to see how disruptive the class would be under my inexperienced guidance. The principal had warned me how disruptive and unruly the class was, and I had seen them chaotically walk down the hall to the lunchroom the day before. I knew that when they walked down the hall under my supervision, I had to prove that I could handle the class; I had to have them in a perfect line.

As we started to line up, the students were all over the place, talking and laughing and nowhere near organized. I had to do something, so I told them that we would not go to lunch until the line was perfectly straight and no one was talking. I soon realized we were going to be there quite a while, as none of the kids gave much weight to my threat. I told them that for every word someone spoke, we were going to wait one complete minute before leaving for lunch. A girl said, "Do what?" and I said, "That will be two extra minutes." Someone yelled, "Ya'll better shut up, because I'm hungry," and I said, "Okay, seven extra minutes, and be glad I didn't count the contractions as two words." After about thirty minutes of this, Mrs. Briley, the head lunchroom lady, came down the hall looking for us. She was quite insistent on sticking to the schedule and she must have thought I had lost my mind. I stuck to my guns, though, and we finally marched down the hall to lunch, forty-five minutes late. I walked at the front of the class, turned backward so I could watch the entire class. Not a single child in the line was making a sound, and as we passed the office, I saw the kids were looking fixedly on something behind me. I couldn't turn around, though, so I had to wait to finally see that they were looking at the principal, who was standing in the office doorway with a dumbfounded expression.

Ever since that day, I have always made sure my classes maintained order outside of the classroom. The way I have them march in lines makes them seem like little soldiers, and some may say that it is militaristic to expect my students to march in such a way, but I think they like the order and structure. The kids seem to enjoy the organization of the line and they are proud of the way they look.

When I first got to PS 83 in Harlem, I saw that the students at the school had been taught to walk in two lines, girls in one and boys in the other, side by side. That added chaos to my single-file line, which in my eyes seemed much easier to manage. Having students stand right beside each other in two lines was just asking for trouble. I've learned, however, that you have to pick your battles, and so I decided not to ask the kids to walk in one line. I don't mind rocking the boat at times, but I decided that this time it would just be easier to keep the two lines. I went with the school's requirement, but I had to add something to it in order to make it more structured. Therefore, I did ask that the kids march in the organized style I requested in my single-file lines, and, also, whenever the two lines would get to a door they were going to enter, I would allow the row closest to the wall to enter first. The other row, standing in a straight line in the center of the hall, would remain there. Then I would say, "Everyone ready . . . and *over*," and instantly, in complete unison, all of the kids would take one step with their right leg and slide to the wall. It was very cool to see the kids move all at once in such a crisp and organized fashion. I would then say, "And . . . *enter*," and they would file into the room. The kids loved it. You may think the kids would be resistant to asking them to be so quiet, disciplined, and orderly, but they actually enjoyed it. Other kids at the school in Harlem asked their teachers if they could line up and enter their rooms in the same way, so some of the other teachers have adopted that format with their classes.

RULE 45

Never cut line. If someone cuts in front of you, do not say or do anything about it. Let it happen, but let me know about it. I will handle the situation. If you fuss with someone who has cut in line, you could get in trouble as well. It's not worth it; just let me know what happened. Please handle all disputes with other classmates in the same manner, by coming to me with any problems before you take matters into your own hands.

I noticed in my first few years of teaching that the kids who seemed to get in the most trouble were the ones fussing with another student who was actually the one who had done something wrong. For example, James may cut Joe in line, but Joe will start to fuss about it and cause a lot of commotion. Joe will usually be angry and loud, and he is the one who will get my attention, and the one who will get in trouble. I wanted to find a way to avoid kids taking matters into their own hands in an inappropriate manner. I started telling the students to come to me with the problem and that I would handle it quietly. I told them that if they fuss or argue, their punishment is going to be worse than that of the person who did something wrong.

I know you may be thinking that it isn't always best for

the students to rely on adults at all times to settle their problems, that kids should learn to handle disputes among themselves, but here is my rationale: Basically, the students know they can't fuss with another student for doing something to them because I am going to punish them even more than the person who did something wrong. Therefore, the students who would normally take matters into their own hands have only two options.

#1.   They can come to me with the problem. You may think that this would be the most common reaction, but in actuality, it isn't. Most kids take the second option . . .

#2.   They can handle the matter themselves, quietly, without being loud or fussing. They know they have to be quiet about it, or I will punish them as well for not handling the situation in an appropriate manner, so they learn to handle matters in a more mature and orderly manner.

When you are dealing with over thirty kids who are in class together all day, five days a week, you have to use whatever works to keep them at peace with each other and on task. Of all the things I have tried, this method seems to be the most effective. The kids discover that it's fine to ask for help when you need it, but more rewarding to solve a problem efficiently on your own, even if you're the only one who knows about it.

⭐ RULE 46

When we go to a movie theater, there will be no talking whatsoever. I don't care how good the movie is or what you want to say to the person beside you, you will not so much as whisper! You will not put your feet on the chair in front of you. If you are going to eat during a movie, you need to eat as quietly as possible. If you purchase candy to eat during the movie, open the wrapper and have it ready before the movie begins; trying to open a bag of candy during a movie is very annoying to others. It is also very rude to leave a cell phone or beeper on during a movie.

It always amazes me when I start to explain how I expect my students to act when we go to the movies that they don't understand why they can't talk when they have a question or when they want to make a comment. They don't understand why they can't open their candy if they are hungry or put their feet on the chairs in front of them if they are uncomfortable. This shows me that the benefits of the behavior I desire out of them isn't as evident to them as it is to me. Once I have told them what is expected, however, they perform in accordance with each thing I have asked of them.

In the popular film *Scary Movie,* there is a scene where a girl is talking on her cell phone throughout the entire movie. Those around her keeping telling her to hush, and she makes the comment, "I paid my money like everybody else in here." That scene is hilarious, but unfortunately that is the type of attitude many people have. Recently I was at the movies with my friend Erica. She knows how I am about manners in the theater, and she assured me she had turned off her cell phone. We were sitting in the crowded theater when I heard Erica whispering. I thought she was talking to the person next to her, and I was about to nudge her to be quiet when I noticed that she was talking on her cell phone. She looked at me and saw that I was not happy, and she whispered to me, "What's wrong? I had it on vibrate."

It may be impossible to live in a world where theater etiquette is observed by all, but hopefully, pointing out to children how they should act will make going to the movies a more positive experience for many people. The first time I took students from Harlem to the movies I spent the entire time getting them to stop talking and to pay attention. Toward the end of that school year, it was a different story. We went to another movie and during the previews there was a family of three children and a mother who were sitting behind us and rambling on and on about one thing or another. I kept trying to catch the mother's eye in order to show her my displeasure with my facial expression, but she wouldn't look my way. My students were sitting there quietly, paying attention and trying to ignore the noise. Finally, just as the previews were ending, a group of them got my attention and said, "Mr. Clark, can we please move?" It sounded like a good idea to me, and all thirty-seven of us stood up, walked down the aisle, and moved to another area of the theater. I'm not sure if that lady took the hint, but that isn't what is important. What's important is that my kids knew the behavior of that lady and her family was wrong. Just months before that, they would have seen it as normal, and they would have been acting the same way.

★ RULE 47

Do not bring Doritos into the school building.

Even though this rule may not make sense to you, and it won't have much relevance to the general public, I didn't feel I could write a book about my fifty-five rules without including it. This is by far the most talked-about rule, and I definitely get more comments and questions about this one than any other. First I will tell you how I explain this rule to my students . . . then I will tell you the truth about this rule.

I tell the students a true story about something that happened when I was young. My mother would buy one bag of Doritos for my sister and me to share as our after-school snack as we watched *The Flintstones*. My sister, Tassie, being greedy, would take out one chip, lick all of the cheese off it, and then place it back in the bag. She knew I would never stick my hand in the bag after that, so she would have it all to herself. As I recount the story I play up the effects it had on me, and I tell my students that to this day I cannot bear to see the sight of a Doritos chip. The truth? Not really. Basically, I just wanted to have a rule that would add character and humor to the list. The little touch of personality adds something unique and quirky to the rules, and the students love it.

This rule definitely causes some commotion and gets the students talking. There will always be students each year who resent not being able to bring Doritos for lunch, but I warn them repeatedly what will happen if they do so. Some will test me, and if I see them with the chips, I will walk over to them wearing a face of disgust, snatch the bag from the table, walk over to the trash can, and bust the bag, sending chips all over the place. Sometimes in class, I will notice a bag of Doritos sticking out of someone's backpack. I will walk to the board and continue to teach like normal.

All of a sudden, I will turn quickly to face the class and say, *"No one move!"* I will then begin to sniff, gliding slowly to the right, slowly to the left. *"Silence!"* My nose will begin to lead me in the correct direction until eventually, *"Aha!"* I will "find" the Doritos, march over to the trash, and crush them, much to the delight of the students and, believe it or not, much to the enjoyment of even the student who has just lost his lunchtime snack. By the way, rumor has it in New York that Mr. Clark can smell Doritos from up to fifty feet away.

I have had teachers use my rules and procedures and later come up to me and say, "Now, Mr. Clark, I have told the kids not to bring Doritos, but I really don't understand why." I usually just laugh and then explain the story. I tell the teachers that they need to develop their own Rule 47 to add their own personality. I explain that they need to make the rules their own.

I recently took a group of former students on a trip to a summer camp. I had taught these students six years previously, but I had remained in contact and was still very close with them. We stopped at a convenience store and each student was allowed to get one drink and one snack. When we got to the van, I noticed that one girl had a bag of Doritos and she had a smirk on her face. I quickly took the bag from her, walked over to a trash can, and smashed the bag between my hands, to the delight of everyone in the van. I said to the girl, "Sabina, why would you get a bag of Doritos?" and she replied, "I knew you were going to do that and it was worth not getting a snack to see it again." Kids love things that are different and unusual, and by performing my "show" to enforce the Doritos rule, I added something unique and memorable to the list.

★ RULE 48

If any child in this school is bothering you, let me know. I am your teacher, and I am here to look after you and protect you. I am not going to let anyone in this school bully you or make you feel uncomfortable. In return, I ask that you not take matters into your own hands; let me deal with the student.

This is a big rule for building morale and a family bond in the class. I want the kids to feel safe in the school, and I want them to see me as someone who will fight for them and stand up for them if the time comes. Some might say, "Mr. Clark, you should let kids fight their own battles." In response I'd say that I feel the kids have enough battles to deal with these days, and if I step in and handle a few of them, so what? I know if I were a kid in school, it would be nice to know I had someone there to take up for me if anyone messed with me.

I remember an incident when I was in sixth grade. I stepped on Lisa Tepper's boots, and she was so angry that she said she was going to get her friends to beat me up. Well, I told my sister, Tassie, who was in high school at the time. The two schools were on the same campus, and the next day Tassie appeared at my classroom door. She told my teacher, Mrs. Woolard, that she had to give Lisa an important message from the office. Lisa walked out in the hall and to this day I have no idea what Tassie said to her, but when Lisa walked back in she was white as a sheet. The message obviously wasn't from the office, it was from my big sister. She had handled the matter, and I never heard one more negative word from Lisa Tepper again.

I want to be that influence in my students' lives. I want them to know they are protected and cared for as long as they are in my class. Whenever they bring it to my attention that another child in the school has bullied them in one form or another, I make sure they know that I will not stand for it and that I am making it a top priority. As soon as possible, I get the two students together, usually outside of the other student's classroom. I remember one time in Harlem when my student Jeremy told me that a kid named Mark was calling him names. During break, I walked Jeremy down the hall and pulled Mark out of his class. I told Mark what I had heard, and then I listened to his version of the story. Mark denied doing anything wrong, but nevertheless, my response was the same. I raised my eyebrow, looked as sternly as possible into Mark's eyes, and said through gritted teeth, "Well, I really don't care what happened. What I *do* care about is that nothing like that *ever* happens again. Now, I am not your teacher, but I am here to tell you right now, you see this student standing here? Well, that is my student in my classroom, and you are not going to talk to him, make fun of him, or bully him, because if you do, you will have to deal with me. Is that clear?" Then I looked at Jeremy, and I gave him the same talk about leaving Mark alone. I told him that if he ever did anything to Mark, he would have to deal with me as well. By speaking to both students, it balances out and seems like I am punishing the boys equally. I wouldn't want it to appear as if I were just taking up for my student and that Jeremy couldn't take care of himself. That could be embarrassing for him and make matters worse.

I never had any problems between Mark and Jeremy again, and I could tell that it meant a lot to Jeremy that I trusted him and took up for him. That type of support from an adult means a lot to a kid, and it goes a long way toward building trust.

in a place where every other male was wearing one. I arranged funding through a business to purchase the tuxedos, but the administration at the school thought it was a waste of money, and the principal was adamant that the money would not be used in that way. She expected me to return the money to the company who had agreed to purchase the suits for the boys, and she said she was not going to change her mind. I stood my ground, however, and with the help of others, we were able to convince the principal that the boys should have the suits. On the night of the ceremony, I knew the struggle had been worth it when I saw the looks on those boys' faces. They were all so excited and proud of themselves to be in the fancy clothes. It was a special moment for them, but if they had been wearing only a shirt and slacks, as the principal had requested, they would have felt out of place and inferior. I never want my students to feel they are substandard to anyone or in any situation.

As a teacher, there are times when you not only have to fight for what you believe in, but also have to stand up for your word. I remember when I began teaching my first class, only a few students consistently brought in their homework each day, and I knew I had to come up with some tactic to teach them to be more responsible. I gave them all a tiny piece of blue paper and told them that anyone who didn't bring it back the next day would get one hour of after-school detention. I know it seems weird, but that is exactly why I did it. I had to find some way to get their attention and to get them in the routine of having an after-school assignment, and if it meant demanding the return of a little piece of blue paper, then so be it. Basically, it was an assignment about responsibility. Of course, the students didn't understand the logic behind it, but I put the fear of a detention in them, and they knew I was serious. In addition, I talked to them about how our class was a team, and told them this was an assignment that we all could accomplish together. I said to the kids, "You don't want to be the one student who forgets the piece of paper and keeps us from having a perfect day of homework."

The next day every single student brought back their tiny pieces of paper. That is, everyone except for one student. That one student, Nancy, just happened to be the brightest, most well-behaved girl in the class. She was a quiet, sweet girl who always had her homework, and I was hesitant to give her a detention; however, the entire class was watching me to see how I was going to handle the situation. If I didn't give Nancy a detention, the students would lose respect for my word. I couldn't go back on what I had said, so I sent the young girl, whose eyes were filled with tears, home with a detention letter.

The next morning when I walked in the school, I was met by my Aunt Carolyn, who was the school's secretary. She looked at me with a frantic expression and said in her southern drawl, "Ron, just go home. Let's call this one a sick day." I asked her what she was talking about, and she informed me that Nancy's mother was in the office and that she was on the warpath. Even though I wanted to go home as my aunt had recommended, I knew I had to face the music and report to the principal's office. I kept telling myself over and over as I walked down the hall, "Ron, what were you thinking? A blue piece of paper as homework was ridiculous!" As I walked in the office, the mother, Mrs. Woodson, shot me a look of hatred, and I was scared to death. We were both called in to sit with the principal, Mrs. Roberson, and she gave each of us the opportunity to voice our concerns. Mrs. Woodson went first. She said that Nancy had cried all night long because of the detention. She said she was a model student, had always completed all of her assignments, and that she had never been in any disciplinary trouble. She felt that punishing her for losing a tiny piece of blue paper was ludicrous. It was obvious this woman was angry, and I was sitting there scared to death of what was going to happen. I could feel tears welling up in my eyes, and I was fighting back the urge to cry. There were several times when Mrs. Roberson could have called on me to speak and I would have just started blubbering like a baby. Luckily, that didn't happen.

After much deliberation, the principal, Mrs. Roberson, suggested that Nancy be given an extra writing assignment instead of attending detention, but I couldn't let that happen. I knew every child in that class was waiting to see if

Nancy was actually going to have to go to detention, and I couldn't back down on my word. I needed those kids to know that I meant what I said. Another suggestion was made to give Nancy silent lunch for a day instead of detention. Again, I stood my ground. Eventually, with the support of Mrs. Roberson and through her soft words of persuasion, we convinced Nancy's mother that the detention assignment must stand. Needless to say, Mrs. Woodson was not happy with it, and she probably still hasn't forgotten it, but it was absolutely necessary in more ways than I could ever explain. Nancy served her detention, and that class went on to have twenty-three days in a row where each child in the class turned in every piece of homework. I turned it into a challenge to see how many days we could all bring in all of our assignments, and it worked. I told them I believed they could do it; I cheered them on, and I jumped on the desks and sang and danced when they had all of their work. Part of the reason that they brought in all of their work was because of the fear of getting a detention; but other teachers had the same policy, but with far less success. The key to my getting those kids to become responsible and bring in their work was that I supported them, and I believed in them. It wouldn't have been possible, however, if I hadn't kept my word about the consequences.

Sometimes it is hard to stand up for what you believe in, and being the only one with a certain vision can be very

lonely. I can only hope that I instill in my students a confidence in who they are and the things they stand for so
that they will have the courage to fight for their beliefs, their
ideas, and their dreams.

★RULE 50

*Be positive and enjoy life. Some things just aren't
worth getting upset over. Keep everything in perspec-
tive and focus on the good in your life.*

I love my parents. They are such wonderful and wise
people. Whenever I have a problem or if something goes
wrong, they have a magical way of showing me that it's never
as bad as it seems. They have always said, "Well, Ron, these
things happen. There's no need to get upset about it; we'll
work through it." I cannot tell you how comforting it is to
hear that.

I remember one time when my mother was taking my
sister and me to school. All of a sudden, smoke started bil-
lowing out of each side of the car hood. Mom pulled over
and got out to see what was going on. This was back in the
good ol' days before cell phones, so Mom had to walk up
the street to a local bar in order to use the phone. It was a
very stressful situation, but my mom stayed calm and positive throughout. Dad came to pick us up, and instead of

cursing or being upset that he had to leave work to come get us or that the car was in need of repair, he just laughed and took us to school and went back to figure out how to get the car to a station. They have always had that type of attitude, no matter what problems we faced, large or small, and they have never gotten negative or disgruntled over issues that are out of their control.

One of the main reasons I love them so much is because of the way they view the world—with tolerance, understanding, and acceptance of all the world has to offer, good and bad. They are such positive people, even in the midst of adversity, and I have tried so hard to adopt that quality myself, and to pass it along to my students.

I recently found out that a former administrator of mine was upset with me because of a comment I made that she had taken the wrong way. I am the type of person who likes everyone to be happy, and I hate the thought of having anyone angry with me. I didn't really want to apologize, because I didn't mean for what I said to be taken the way she perceived it. It was bothering me, though, and when I asked my mother for advice, she told me that I should either write a letter or call the person and explain the situation. I decided to do both. First I wrote a letter, and later I called. Neither worked to smooth over the situation, as the administrator remained cold and distant. It continued to bother me, and I again asked my mother for advice, and she told me something very wise. She said, "Ron, you have taken the pressure off yourself. You did the right thing; you called and made your peace. Now the burden is not on you anymore, it is on her. If she chooses to live with it, then let her, but I want you to stop worrying about it."

My mother was right. We can't let things bother us to the point that they make us sick. We have to realize there are some things we can't change, and there are times when there are no easy solutions. It is best to deal with those situations the best we can, take the pressure off of ourselves, and move on.

★ RULE 51

Live so that you will never have regrets. If there is something you want to do, do it! Never let fear, doubt, or other obstacles stand in your way. If there is something you want, fight for it with all of your heart. If there is something you want to do, go for it and don't stop until you make it happen. If there is something you want to be, do whatever is necessary in order to live out that dream.

My greatest fear is that I am going to have regrets about the way I have led my life. When I was twenty-one years old, I found out that I had a family member I had never met. I desperately wanted to meet the person after I found out, but I could not get up the courage to do so. After months and months of chickening out, I finally made plans to go and see the person on the following Monday. Unfortunately, he died the Sunday before I was supposed to go see him. I was absolutely devastated. All of the times I was too scared to go meet him came flooding back to me, and I was very hard on myself for not having had the guts to talk to him. At that moment, I realized that even though I never met the man, he taught me one of the greatest lessons of my life, and that is to live so that I won't regret my choices or decisions. That is one of the main reasons why I have lived my life the way I have. Before his death, I had always wanted to travel, but I was terrified to get on a plane. After the incident, however, I realized that I never wanted to regret anything again, and I started traveling extensively, living in London, backpacking across Europe, spending time in Japan. I am so thankful I did so. I know if I looked back on my life and I hadn't had my adventures and travels, I would have felt my life was only half lived.

I tell my students that story, as well as others like it, because I want them to truly understand that they have got to make the most of their lives and not let anything stand in the way of their dreams.

⭐ RULE 52

Accept that you are going to make mistakes.
Learn from them and move on.

We are only human, and parents, teachers, and students alike will all do things they will regret. I made mistakes my first year of teaching, I made mistakes my seventh year of teaching, and I'm sure I'll make mistakes my thirtieth year of teaching. When it happens, you can't beat yourself up over it. You have to pick yourself up, learn from the experience, and move on.

The class of students I took over in my first year of teaching was a very hard group to discipline. To get them to focus and pay attention during lessons, I had to arrange the room so Steve couldn't see Bill and Aaron couldn't see Lakisha, and so on. I even had a partition in the corner where I would make an extremely rowdy student go and stand. One day around 1:30 P.M., I made a student named Jermaine stand behind that partition. I went on teaching and got really into it, and before I knew it the bell rang, and it was time for the students to go home. They were dismissed and I sat at my desk, completely exhausted. I started grading papers, and around 3:15 P.M. I heard a BOOM!! I jumped out of the seat and looked in the corner to see Jermaine lying on the floor. He had fallen asleep against the wall and had slipped and knocked down the whole partition. I don't know who was scared more, me or Jermaine! I got him up and drove him home, and I swore I would never put anyone behind that partition again.

Another mistake I made that year involved another teacher at the school. Her name was Mrs. Bitterson, and her classroom was right across the hall from mine. She was a much older teacher, approaching retirement, and there was no doubt about it, she didn't approve of my teaching methods. She was especially angry with me because she was the fourth-grade teacher, and she thought I was making fifth grade look too much like fun. She claimed that her students couldn't concentrate because they were too concerned with what was going on in my class across the way. We had several meetings with the principal about this, but none of the meetings turned out as Mrs. Bitterson had hoped. The principal supported me and my techniques, and Mrs. Bitterson would always make some snide remark like, "Well, I knew you were going to take up for him; he's your *golden boy!*" She ended up leaving each meeting with more and more resentment toward me.

One afternoon Mrs. Bitterson walked by my door with her class and threw a tennis ball into the room. I had started a tennis team with my students, and apparently I had left one of the balls on the playground. She stuck her head in my room and stated, "Mr. Clark, YOU left this on the playground and one of my students could have tripped on it and been injured, and YOU could have been taken to court. How would you like THAT?" I replied, "Well, you just threw that same ball in my classroom, and you could have hit one of my students in the eye, and YOU could have been the one in court. How would YOU like THAT?" I realize now that this was a horrible response, and I should have handled the situation much differently, but I was about to head into a horrid spiral of events with Mrs. Bitterson, and I didn't have the experience to know how to get myself out of it.

Later that afternoon, there was a knock at my door. I answered it, but the only thing I saw was a green package sitting on the floor. I picked it up and carried it into the room. I said with a big grin, "Look, kids, someone's given us a present." As I opened it, moths and crickets sprang out, and worms, slugs, and other bugs fell to the floor. The package was on Tamarus's desk and that poor kid just about had a heart attack, and I was not far from it. It contained no name, but it was obvious that it was from Mrs. Bitterson, who loved science and had all types of insects and animals in her room. My kids definitely took it as a "slam" on them as well, and they were anxious to get revenge. I assured them that our day would come and that we would have our revenge.

The next day, while Mrs. Bitterson's class was in the lunchroom, my students and I got an onion that we had used earlier in an experiment. We cut the onion in half and, with caution and slyness to rival that of James Bond (I really hammed it up for the kids' amusement), I snuck into Mrs. Bitterson's room and wedged the pieces into the back of her top drawer.

About two weeks passed, and I had completely forgotten about the onion. Then, one day, I noticed Mrs. Bitterson spraying her strawberry mist air freshener around her desk. (Lord knows she loved that strawberry mist.) I walked in her room and asked her what she was doing. She replied in her usual scratchy tone, "Something in here stinks, and I can't find it." Mrs. Bitterson loved a cotton plant that was hanging above her desk, and so out of pure cruelty I said, "Hmm, I think it's your cotton plant." She darted back at me, "You don't know what you're talking about, Golden Boy; cotton plants don't stink!" Later that afternoon, I saw her carrying the plant to the Dumpster. Apparently, she was beginning to believe I was right about where the smell was coming from. I was really enjoying this joke, until days later when I left the school to head home. When I walked out to my car, it had been smeared from bumper to bumper with pieces of onion. Bless her heart, she had finally found that onion.

I was not going to let her get the last word, so I scraped the onion off my car and took it home. I then pureed the pieces and put it in a container. The next morning, I made sure I was the first to arrive at school. I took the onion liquid and poured it into Mrs. Bitterson's strawberry mist bottle. I then sprayed it all over her room.

When she walked into her class, she stopped abruptly; she knew I had put the onion somewhere, but for the life of her she couldn't find exactly where the smell was coming from. I had to suppress my laughter all morning as she had her kids turning the room upside down in an attempt to find the onion. All the while, she stormed from one end of the room to the other, spraying that "strawberry mist" with all her might.

It wasn't until after that event that a teacher at the school, Mrs. Zurich, sat me down and told me some things about Mrs. Bitterson that I hadn't known. She was really a very kind and generous woman, but because of certain things that had happened in her life, she didn't quite have the zest and energy that she once had for education. Mrs. Zurich said that one of the reasons Mrs. Bitterson did not like me was because she wanted to teach just like me, but she didn't know how. Also, Mrs. Bitterson wanted the kids to like her, just as we all do, but she didn't know how to make that happen. Mrs. Zurich really opened my eyes, and I soon realized that there were a number of ways I could have turned my experience with Mrs. Bitterson into a positive one. I could have teamed up with Mrs. Bitterson to do a science project with both of our classes. I will openly admit that science is my worst subject, and I sure could have used the help. I also could have gone to Mrs. Bitterson for help with things that I usually asked other teachers about.

I could have made her feel like she was needed. I could have respected her. Instead, I made a bad situation worse, but I learned from my mistakes.

At times, there are going to be conflicts between teachers or any two people working together. Sometimes, it is best to swallow a little pride and smooth the situation over. Asking a coworker for help or advice is a huge compliment, and it can go a long way in repairing tense relationships. Since the situation with Mrs. Bitterson, I have learned to appreciate that all teachers have advice, skills, and talent that can make all of us better teachers. We just have to learn to let each other know that we appreciate what we can learn from each other and that there is mutual respect.

An additional detriment of not getting along with co-teachers is the impact it has on the students. One day after the onion fiasco, I saw Mrs. Bitterson telling one of my students to stop running down the hall. He looked at her like she was crazy and he kept right on going. I, of course, caught up with him and gave him a lecture he wouldn't soon forget, but the point is, he had no respect for Mrs. Bitterson, and that came as a result of my treatment and opinion of her. When there is tension between teachers, the students will feel it, and it will cause them to be uncomfortable. Kids these days are witness to enough hostility; they shouldn't have to endure it at school as well. On the flip side, when teachers get along and like each other, the students feel more at peace and will perform better in that type of environment. My co-teacher Barbara Jones and I got along so well. We were always laughing, giving high-fives and supporting each other. The students loved to be around us and they thrived when they were with us. That is the type of environment we should make for our kids.

Making mistakes such as leaving kids in corners or being childish with vegetables are part of life, and no matter how old or experienced we are, they will still happen. One thing for sure, though, is that with experience, there are far fewer mistakes. The longer I teach, the fewer errors I make, and as the years pass, when I do make a slipup, I am much more equipped to handle it.

Mistakes will happen. Accept it and learn from them.

★ RULE 53

No matter what the circumstances, always be honest. Even if you have done something wrong, it is best to admit it to me, because I will respect that, and oftentimes I will forget any disciplinary measures because of your honesty.

One day a parent came to my classroom door and asked to speak to me in the hall. As I stepped outside, I told the class to get ready for lunch and *not* to say a word. I talked to the parent for a couple of minutes, and then I went back in the class and told the students to line up. As the kids passed me in the line, many of them were whispering out of the side of their mouths, "Candy and Grier were talking." I didn't say anything to the culprits at that time, but as Candy and Grier walked out of the room I asked them to stand over to the side so I could talk to them. I leaned down and looked them in the eyes as I said, "Girls, I know I can count on you two. Can you please tell me if *anyone* in the room was talking while I was in the hall." Candy responded as her hair bobbed from side to side by saying, "*Oh no, Mr. Clark,* you would have been *soooo* proud of everyone. We just were so busy getting ready for lunch that no one had a chance to talk at all." I looked her dead in the eyes and said, "Are you sure, Candy?" and she answered, "*Oh yes, Mr. Clark.* I would *never* lie, because my mom taught me lying is wrong, and I respect you too much to lie to you, and besides, *I've* read the Bible." Well, I then put on my all-hell-is-about-to-break-loose face and I said, "*Well, ladies,* let me tell you a little something, when I was outside, I could hear both of you talking!" Grier turned white as a sheet and she said, "*Oh I am so sorry,* Mr. Clark, I *was* talking." I said, "Well, thank you for being honest, Grier, go on to the lunchroom." Immediately, Candy sprang into action: "*Oh, Mr. Clark,* I am sorry, but I was talking too. Can I go to the

the lunchroom. A group of students told me that she broke into the line, so I walked over to where she was standing in line and asked her if it was true. Her mouth said, "No," but her eyes were screaming, "Yep!" I said, "Okay, Antoinkena, I am going to ask you again, and this time I want the truth. Did you jump line?" Again she replied, *"No!"* I could have easily told her to go to the back of the line as punishment, but I wanted more; I wanted her to admit it. I bent down and got level with her face and I looked as hard into her eyes as I could as I said, "Antoinkena, until you admit to me that you broke line, no one in this line is going to eat." Well, fifteen minutes later she was still standing there and there were now three classes of angry, hungry students standing behind her. We were at a standoff and I knew I had to do something. I decided to try one last thing. I looked her right in the eyes and said, "Antoinkena Wallace, you better tell the truth and let the Lord love you." That is a popular southern expression, and for Antoinkena, being from an area where religion is an integral part of many of the students' lives, it hit home. Her eyes got big as saucers and she said, quick as lightning, "I did it." I simply said, "Thank you for telling the truth. Now go eat."

Believe it or not, I enjoy working with students who have had behavior problems in the past or have a lot of personal issues they are dealing with. Antoinkena definitely fell into that category, and we had an instant connection. I admired her spunk, her spirit, and her determination, where others had been annoyed or appalled by it. I took Antoinkena under my wing and got her involved with a tennis team I started at the school. Soon, her whole attitude began to change, and she became pleasant and much more respectful to all of the teachers around the school. I will never forget the joy I got from working with Antoinkena and seeing the difference I was able to make in her life. She will be one of my favorite students forever, and that's the truth.

★ RULE 54

> *Carpe diem. You only live today once, so don't waste it. Life is made up of special moments, many of which happen when caution is thrown to the wind and people take action and seize the day.*

This rule sounds very similar to Rule 51, but they are really two very different things in my eyes and deserve to be separate lessons. Rule 51 is about living the life you want to lead. This rule, carpe diem, is about living each day to the fullest and appreciating each moment.

My students must hear this a thousand times a year. It is part of who I am as a teacher and a person; it is the way I live my life and it is my wish for my students that they can learn how important it is to make the most of each and

every day of their lives. I recently took a group of nine students from Harlem to North Carolina for a week. I just
packed them in a van and we took off for a trip that I know
changed their lives forever. Before we left New York, I said
to the kids, "We are going to make the most of this week.
We are going to live each day to the fullest, and anything you
get the chance to do in North Carolina, I want you to do it;
even if it is new or different or scary, I want you to *go for it*!" I
had them make a pact with me that during the week we
would all live up to the carpe diem philosophy, and during
that week, they didn't let me down. Kids who were afraid
of heights were climbing rock walls, kids who had never
been in water were learning to water-ski, and kids who had
never eaten pig at a hog cooking were asking if they could
eat the tongue . . . and they did! It was a wild week of adventure, fun, and new experiences. We finished off the week
at an amusement park. Now, I do not like roller coasters;
they scare me to death, and I was going to break the pact
because of my fear. Can you believe it, I was going to be
the one to let the group down and not live up to my own
advice? I couldn't help it, I was just so terrified. Then one
of my students looked at me and quoted a line I had said
to him many times before, "Mr. Clark, you better get busy
living, or get busy dying."

My own words, back in my face—and they worked. I
found myself, with the kids at my side, getting on each and

every ride. I had never really enjoyed amusement parks before that day, but because I abandoned all fear, and got busy living, I loved every minute of it. I was living. That week, we were all living.

How wonderful it would be to live an entire life with such freedom to try new things, experience the unknown, and face our fears. It is hard for many adults to step out there and take those chances, but kids are more willing to release their inhibitions and truly live life. If we can teach them to embrace that feeling when they are young, hopefully it will stay with them for the rest of their lives.

★ RULE 55

Be the best person you can be.

Throughout life, you are going to be lonely at times, you are going to have your heart broken on occasion, and you are going to feel as if something is missing from your life. No life is lived without some amount of pain and heartache. No matter how bad things get, however, make sure you are always developing into the kind of person you want to be, and the kind of person others will want to be around. It is important not to let external factors keep you from developing who you are and the person you are trying to become. Always make sure there are seven things in your life at all times: laughter, family, adventure, good food, challenge, change, and the quest for knowledge. With all of those things, you will grow, enjoy life, and become the type of person you can be proud of. You will also be in a better position to help others, give advice, and learn from your mistakes, because you will be a stronger, healthier, and happier person.

A FEW TIPS FOR DEALING WITH CHILDREN

Journal entry:

I can't sleep. Tomorrow is the first day of school, it's 3:30 a.m., and I am too nervous to get any rest. Even if I do fall asleep, I will probably have the dream again where I realize I have left my class alone somewhere in the school, and I can't find them. I just keep running up and down the halls, terrified because I have left them unsupervised. I finally find the kids, and they have been in my class the entire time. I was the one who was lost, and I was in the wrong place, not the students. As I walk in, I see that the principal has discovered the unattended class, and she is standing at the front of the room with her arms crossed with a disgruntled expression on her face.

NIGHTMARE!

I know that dream is all about my fear that I am going to fail my students, that I am not going to be there for them. I am afraid the students won't like me, that they aren't going to listen to me, and that I won't be able to reach them. I am scared to death that I am going to fail . . .

That is an actual excerpt from my journal. You would probably think I wrote it on the night before my first day as a teacher, but it was actually written just before the first day of my seventh year in the classroom. Working with kids is nerve-racking. No matter how much practice or experience you have, there will always be worries and the fear that you will do something wrong. That is understandable, because there is no responsibility greater than raising children. Whether you are a parent, a teacher, a counselor, or a member of the community, you face the task of setting a positive example for children, motivating them to succeed, and making a difference in their lives.

During my years of working with students and all we went through together, I learned a lot about what makes kids tick and what methods are best when it comes to handling different situations. One thing I know for certain is that when you work with kids, you have to be clever. Overall, there are four universal truths I have gathered about kids.

#1. Kids need and like structure.

Students like to feel they are safe and that there is a figure of authority in control. I have seen teachers, as well as parents, make the mistake of being too lenient in order to win the affection of children. First-year teachers have said to me that they don't want to be too strict, because they want the students to like them. In the beginning, I think students do like those teachers, but in the end, they have no respect for them. The best result is to have students who like you *and* respect you. In order to do that, you have to create structure in the classroom, you have to have clear, defined rules, and you have to make the students feel safe and comfortable.

#2. Kids will work hard for you, if they like who you are as a person.

Having a good discipline program will garner respect, but you may still have kids who do not particularly like you. Getting kids to like you can be quite a task. During the summer, before I ever meet my new class of students, I send them letters so that they will already know about me and my personality before the first day of school. I make sure to include lots of pictures in the letter that show I like to have fun and do exciting things. On the first day of school, I give the kids a brief slide show of pictures of me and places I have traveled. I also have slides that show me when I was their age. I want the kids to immediately make a connection to me; I want them to see I am real and more than just their teacher.

Another tactic I use to get kids to like me is to do anything to get their attention, no matter how foolish it makes me look or how embarrassing it may be. I am shameless when I am with them. Sacrificing a little dignity can go a long way when you are trying to win over students. I can remember how my mother used to tuck me in each night when I was little. She would go to take off my socks, then act like they were impossible to get off. She would pull and pull and they would stretch and stretch. The facial expressions she would make were the funniest things I had ever seen in my life. In the end, the socks would fly off and she would tumble onto the bed. Did she look like a fool doing that? Yes. Did I love her for it? Most definitely. When I stand in front of the classroom, I let down my guard. I have no inhibitions, I put on those funny faces, I tumble to the floor, and I am willing to do whatever it takes to get through to the students.

One final thing I do to get kids to like me might be seen as strange. I give them a speech on the first day of school that goes something like this:

"I don't care if you don't like me. I couldn't care less. I am not here to be friends with any of you either. I have plenty of friends and I don't need any more. I don't care if you get mad and call me bad names in your mind. You are more than welcome to do that, because my objective here isn't to have you like me; it's to have you learn. I care about each and every one of you, and I am dedicated and driven to giving you the best education possible. I want each of you to know that I am going to do whatever it takes to make that happen, and nothing is going to stand in my way."

That may seem a bit harsh, but it is an important speech for many reasons. First, it's letting the kids know they are not going to get away with foolishness in the classroom, but at the same time, they know I care about them and that I am driven and dedicated to giving them the best education possible. It shows the kids where my priorities are, and it lays the groundwork for the type of year we are going to have. The funny thing about the speech, though, is that I am telling them just as hard as I can that I don't care if they don't like me, but at the same time, I am working my butt off to be the type of teacher they will like. I'm giving slide shows, dancing, standing on chairs, singing, acting, you name it.

Do I want the kids to like me? Yes, it is absolutely necessary. Do I let them know that? No. When kids know you want them to like you, you are giving them powerful ammunition to use against you, and in the end they could, and probably will, take advantage of that. Telling them the "story" of how you couldn't care less if they like you or not gives you the upper hand. You can't discipline kids and not love them, and you can't love them and not discipline them. The two must go hand in hand.

#3. Kids like to know what is expected of them.

It's unrealistic to expect kids to automatically behave exactly as you hope they will. Kids are kids, and many actions that may seem like common sense to us will seem foreign to them. I have found that no matter who the child is, if you explain exactly what you want from him and exactly how you hope he will act, then he will try his best to perform up to your standards. Often, children who are in trouble will ask, "What did I do?" or say, "I didn't do anything." These kids honestly don't understand what they did wrong, and if they don't understand that their action was inappropriate, then how were they supposed to know not to do it in the first place? We have to be specific when we tell kids what we expect from them. We have to spell it out clearly so that there is no question in the children's minds when it comes to what is right or wrong.

During my first couple of years as a teacher, I would see a child do something wrong, and I would immediately give punishments such as silent lunch or no recess. Kids like Tyquad Johnson—who when punished scrunched up his face each and every time as if he were constipated—would angrily take the disciplinary action. I learned after a while that no lesson was really being learned in these cases. Often, the kids didn't even understand why their actions made me so upset. They didn't understand what they had done wrong. I eventually started talking one-on-one with kids about what had happened. One of the first things I always say is, "Tell me what you think you did wrong," or "Tell me why you think I am upset." It is always very advantageous to hear the kid's take on the situation. Most always you will have two completely different views about what happened, and if you don't take the time to explain why you are upset, then the student will continue to harbor anger or resentment toward you for the punishment. Kids definitely want to know what is expected of them, and when they are doing something wrong, it is important to explain why their actions were inappropriate to avoid it happening again.

#4. Kids like to know they are cared for.

In my first year of teaching, there was a child named Raymond who was a very disrespectful and disruptive child. In the classroom he was a leader to other students, and the chaos he created affected the climate of the entire class. I knew if I could find a way to reach him that it would go a long way in terms of helping to control the entire class. One Friday afternoon, Raymond told me in a very cocky tone that he wasn't going to complete his weekend homework, because he had basketball games to play on Saturday and Sunday in the recreation league. I didn't argue with him. Instead, I found out where the games were going to be played and I attended the games. When Raymond saw me, he was shocked and asked what I was doing there. I told him I was there to cheer him on, and he couldn't believe it. Throughout the games, every time he made a shot, dribbled the ball, made a steal, or got a rebound, he would glance over to see if I was watching. My being there that day meant a great deal to Raymond, and that Monday he came in with all of his homework completed, neat and correct. In fact, Raymond turned into a model student. He became respectful and hardworking, and he no longer was a source of negative leadership; on the contrary, he became a positive role model for the rest of the class. The previous year he had scored better than only 16 percent of all fourth graders in the state on the end-of-grade reading test. At the end of the fifth-grade year, he scored better than 68 percent of all fifth graders. That improvement came simply because I showed him that I cared for him, and that sparked him to perform.

It seems simple, and it is. Kids want to know you care for them. Before they are willing to invest effort in what you are saying, they want to know you are willing to make an investment in them. Once you have done that, dealing with kids is a much easier, more productive, and more meaningful experience.

TIPS FOR DEALING
WITH PARENTS

In order for a classroom discipline plan to work, it is imperative that you have the support of the parents. Their backing and belief in your judgment will go a long way in making for an enjoyable and hassle-free year. However, if the right relationship isn't developed, dealing with parents can honestly be one of the worst parts of being a teacher. I, for one, have dozens of personal horror stories. Fortunately, most of them happened in my first couple of years of teaching, and I was able to learn from them and change the way I interacted with parents; however, no matter how much practice you have or how well you build a relationship with parents, in the end, problems will inevitably arise.

In my first year of teaching, there was a parent, Mrs. Cleveland, who felt I was far too strict with her son. She ranted and raved and met with the principal, but all of her efforts got her nowhere. While watching TV one afternoon, she saw a commercial that said, "If you have an emergency, call 911." Feeling her dilemma had reached emergency status, she called 911 and reported me. The police, having to follow through with the call, showed up at my classroom door. I just about fell out when they told me why they were there. Mrs. Cleveland was called to the school, and she met with the principal, the police, and the guidance counselor, and they informed her why it was not appropriate to call 911 because she was unhappy with her child's teacher.

I recall a student in my class, named Darnell, who was a major discipline problem. I had managed to contact all of my students' parents, but his phone was disconnected, and I wasn't sure he was giving his mother any of the messages I was sending home with him. Finally, after weeks of trying, I got his mother on the phone. The conversation went something like this:

Mrs. Cob: Hello.

Me: May I speak with Mrs. Cob?

Mrs. Cob: Who's this?

Me: This is Mr. Clark, Darnell's teacher.

Mrs. Cob: WHO?

Me: I am Mr. Clark, Darnell's teacher.

Mrs. Cob: Uh-huh, what has he done?

Me: Well, let me tell you. He has been fighting with other kids, he spit on one girl, he won't pay attention, he hasn't had any of his homework, and I am tired of it.

Mrs. Cob: Well, you know what? He does the same types of things when he is at home with me and I have to deal with it while he's here, so you deal with him while he's there. *Click.*

That conversation may sound unbelievable, but I have encountered several parents who had that same mentality. Some see school as an extended day care service. Others view teachers as the help. It is a constant struggle to gain respect for teachers. I actually learned a lot from the conversation with Mrs. Cob, and the next year when I encountered a similar problem with a very unruly child named Trey, I handled the situation quite differently.

Mrs. Banks: Hello.

Me: Can I speak with Mrs. Banks?

Mrs. Banks: Who's this?

Me: This is Mr. Clark, Trey's teacher.

Mrs. Banks: Uh-huh, what did he do now?

Me: Actually, I was just calling to let you know how much I am enjoying having Trey in class. He gets very excited about learning and he brings a lot of energy to classroom discussions.

Mrs. Banks: Really?

Me: Oh yes, and I told him today, I said, "Trey, you always have such nice manners. I can

Mrs. Banks: tell your mother really raised you well," and it was then that I decided to call you to thank you in person for the great job you have done with Trey.

Mrs. Banks: For real? He ain't in no trouble?

Me: Oh no, he is a pleasure to teach. It was nice talking with you, and I'll be in touch.

Mrs. Banks: Okay . . . well . . . good night, Mr. Clark.

Okay, I was lying through my teeth there, but there was a method to my madness. In all honesty, Trey was driving me out of my mind, and I was at my wit's end with him. The next morning after the call, he walked into the class and gave me a look like, "What in the world are you thinking?" I am sure when he heard his mother had spoken to me that he assumed he was in trouble, but then she probably praised him for doing such a good job. I bet he was thinking, "Hey, I can be downright horrible in here, and he's not even gonna tell my mom." Little did he know . . .

I waited three agonizing days and then I called again.

Mrs. Banks: Hello.

Me: Hey, Mrs. Banks, this is Mr. Clark. How are you doing?

Mrs. Banks: Oh, I'm doing good. How 'bout you?

Me: I'm fine, but I burned my fried chicken tonight.

Mrs. Banks:	No you didn't!
Me:	Yes I did! . . . Listen, I know you are going to be shocked when I tell you this, because, quite honestly, it has really surprised me.
Mrs. Banks:	What is it?
Me:	Well, Trey has actually been acting up a little bit in class, and I just couldn't believe it.
Mrs. Banks:	What has he been doing?
Me:	Well, he hasn't been doing all of his work and he has been bothering other students. Finally today I just called him out in the hall and I said to him, "Trey, I cannot believe your behavior today. You come from such a good family, and your mother has worked so hard with you and done such a good job of raising you. When you are acting out in class, you are really disrespecting her." And you know what? He acted like he didn't even care about that.
Mrs. Banks:	Hold on, Mr. Clark . . . *Trey!! Get your butt in here right now!!!*

I had to suffer through a few days of Trey's driving me crazy and thinking he had gotten the best of me, but in the end, I had a direct link to his mother, who stayed on him and worked with me to keep him on track for the rest of the year. The main thing I learned from that first phone call with Trey's mom is that, no matter what, the first contact with the parent has got to be a positive one.

As I said, even after years of working with parents, there will still be times when conflicts arise. The second year I was teaching in Harlem, there was a father who scared the crap out of me. I began to think his favorite pastime was leaving threatening messages on my answering machine. If he thought I gave his daughter, Francisca, too much home-work, I was going to have to hear about how he could twist my body in three different directions. I am not even going to lie about it, I avoided that man at all costs, but there were, unfortunately, times when I had to meet with him. Once I took Francisca on a field trip with five other stu-dents. I took them out to eat in a nice restaurant and to the movies, and I paid for the entire trip. All I asked of the parents was that they pick up their children at the subway stop at 8:00 P.M. Well, at 8:30 P.M., I was still sitting there with Francisca. I got her to call home on the pay phone, and fifteen minutes later her parents showed up, and they were furious. They thought that I was going to walk each child home. I explained to them how it stated on the per-mission slip they signed that they were to pick her up at the station. Their only defense was that they hadn't read it, and that they thought it was extremely rude and unprofessional that I had not taken each child home.

You may wonder why I would pick Francisca to go on a trip like that in the first place. Well, she was an absolutely wonderful student and person, and I knew she needed to have that type of experience. She was probably one of the most gifted students I have ever taught. Fortunately for her, her parents, although fond of threatening me at every turn, were also willing to allow me to take Francisca on trips. They did want the best for her, and they knew that the trips and activities I was getting her involved in were going to benefit her in many ways. They even allowed me to take her, along with a group of eight other students, on a week-long trip to North Carolina. Francisca absorbed every experience on that trip, from learning to water-ski to rolling down sand dunes, and from riding four-wheelers to attending a pig pickin'—a southern tradition. She really came to life that week, and I know the experience will live with her forever. Now, the trip was at no cost to her parents, and I expected them to at least show some appreciation when I returned Francisca home. However, her father misunderstood the time of arrival and had to wait for us at the school for hours before we arrived. The father was furious with me, and he proceeded to let me know, in front of the other parents, how inconvenienced he had been by having to wait there for us and that I should learn to get my act together. He included several examples of profanity in his monologue. I just tried to keep the picture in my mind of Francisca laughing as she rolled down those sand dunes as I got in the van and drove away.

Why am I sharing these horrible stories? Well, to be

honest, whenever I have problems with parents like the ones I have mentioned, the one thing that seems to make me feel better is listening to other teachers share similar stories. It helps to know that others encounter the same type of parents and that it is inevitable. Hopefully, by sharing some of my trials, it will help others when they have to face their own difficult situations.

I have, by an overwhelming percentage, far more stories of parents who were supportive, helpful, and a pleasure to work with. I have had parents as chaperones on trips who were so wonderful and supportive of me that it was overwhelming what they were willing to put up with and the tasks they were willing to take on in order to help out. I have called parents at 9:00 P.M. in order to organize an emergency bake sale for the next day for one reason or another, and they would show up at my door the next morning holding trays of cupcakes. I asked one parent to drive an hour away to pick up 500 dozen doughnuts in her minivan, and she did, but doughnut glaze seeped all over her seats. She told me it was fine, and the next time we sold doughnuts, she was the first one to volunteer to pick them up again. The best thing I think parents can do for me, however, is to give me their trust. No matter how much the students like you, there are going to be times when they feel they have been "done wrong." A lower score than they expected, a punishment they deem too harsh, or simply by not calling on them enough to answer questions can give kids enough reason to despise the ground you walk on. I absolutely loved my sixth-grade teacher, Mrs. Woolard. She is one of my favorite teachers of all time; however, when I recently read back through my sixth-grade diary she had us keep, I found one passage where I wrote: "Today was horrible. I raised my hand over and over and Mrs. Woolard called on other students first. I hate that woman!" You have to love the mind of a sixth grader.

The wonderful thing about kids, though, is that those feelings usually only last a few hours, and then they love you again. The problem is, before that time runs out, they usually have shared with their parents how horrible a teacher you are. This is where the trust comes into play. I tell the parents at the beginning of the year to expect their kids to say I am too harsh or to complain about the amount of work I assign. I also ask them to trust in me that I know what I am doing. The parents who understand that are a blessing, but there are some who will believe whatever their child says and will be quick to jump to his or her defense. Many times they will call and won't even ask me for my side of the story. They will assume that events happened in exactly the way their child stated. Again, these parents, for the most part, are in the minority, and I have thoroughly enjoyed working with numerous parents who made my job and my life a lot easier.

There are five things I would like to ask of the parents of my students:

#1.   If you feel there is problem with me or my teaching, do not call the principal. Call me first and give me the chance to discuss the concerns with you.

#2.   If you need to talk to me, send a note with your child. I'll write back and we can arrange a time to meet. Do not show up at the classroom door unannounced for a conference.

#3.   Do not allow your child to be late or miss school for anything other than sickness or a death in the family. Allowing your child to miss school because he needs to get a haircut or go clothes shopping with you is sending the wrong message to children.

#4.   Realize that your child is one of many I teach each day, and that it is not always possible to address each and every need he or she may have. The sole responsibility of educating children is not the teacher's alone; it is the parents' as well.

#5.   Trust me that I know what I am doing.

I have never voiced these requests to my students' parents, but for the most part, I believe most of them know these things innately. It's the ones who don't that you have to worry about, and I can only offer six points of advice where they are concerned:

#1.   Make sure the initial contact with parents is a positive one, with no negativity at all.

#2.   Any time you talk with parents, make sure the first comment about their child's performance in the classroom is a positive one. (John might have failed every class, but if he did a good job on an art project, talk about that first.)

#3.   Wear professional attire. I have found that when I dress in a suit and tie, the students and their parents treat me with more respect. During class, I have far fewer discipline problems, and when talking with parents, their overall tone is more respectful and cooperative. Besides, teachers who want to be treated like professionals should dress and act like professionals.

#4. Send notes home or call parents out of the blue to tell them something good their child did. (When I have done that, parents always comment about how no teacher ever did that before. Parents love to hear good things about their kids, and it will go a long way toward building a good relationship between you and the parents.)

#5. Take every possible opportunity to thank parents. If they donate supplies to the class, help with a party, chaperone a trip, or make any other contribution to the class, send them a thank-you note. It will make them feel appreciated, and they will be far more likely to help out in the future.

#6. If a parent is extremely difficult to get along with, don't be afraid to schedule a meeting with the principal where you can express your concerns. If that doesn't work, avoid that parent like the plague. Any contact with him or her should be made through written notes. Don't put yourself through the torture.

TIPS FOR SETTING PUNISHMENTS AND REWARDS

When developing consequences, I tried to make them as simple and as easy for me to deliver as possible. I didn't want to get bogged down with having to punish students and putting stars by names or keeping up with stickers on charts on their desks. I wanted it to be quick and easy. Therefore, I decided that the most efficient way would be that if a student breaks a rule, his name is placed on the board; this is only a warning. A second time I have to reprimand a student he receives a check. For each additional infraction, additional checks are given, and the consequences are as follows:

Name on Board
Warning, no consequences other than the name being on the board.

One Check

At lunchtime, I look on the board and make a note of the students and how many checks each one has. All students who have at least one check will have to sit with me at lunch. I usually pick a table that is off to the side. No talking, whatsoever, is allowed. If a student laughs or says one word, he will be given another day of silent lunch.

Two Checks

Students with two checks will lose recess. If the students go to recess with another teacher, I keep the punished students in the room with me. If I go outside with the class, I instruct the students who lost their recess to sit along the side of the fence. If there is no recess because of rain, the students will lose part of their gym time. Some parents may say it is cruel to take away recess from kids, but I would say to them, "Listen, we are fighting in the trenches here. Teaching isn't easy, and sometimes we have to do what is necessary to get the kids to behave."

Before I actually started teaching the class myself, I watched Mrs. Waddle take away kids' recess periods and I thought, "That monster." Two weeks later I found myself saying, after a student had stuck another kid with a pencil after being warned three times not to, *"All right, Danyell, you just lost your recess!"* It is a different world when you are the teacher and you are doing whatever it takes to maintain order in that classroom.

detention, so the parents didn't mind. In North Carolina, however, the school was in a rural area and having students stay until 4:00 meant the parents would have to make a special trip to drive to the school to pick up their child. Some parents saw this as an inconvenience to them and not the student. I felt that if the child wasn't prepared for school each day, some of the responsibility should fall on the parent, and therefore I liked the punishment. If the parents, however, are absolutely adamant about the child not serving detention, then I find a punishment that is equally effective. For example, I will make a deal with the parent that the student will be assigned a three-page report on a certain topic, usually one that deals with a subject we are studying in school. The child will be given two days to complete the report. The deal is, if it is not completed, then the child will have to serve the day of detention. About 90 percent of the time the report is not completed, and the parent has to concede and allow the child to stay for detention. If you have to substitute punishments, you *must* make sure it is something comparable in terms of the students not wanting to do it. If students see that others are not having to deal with the consequences, then you have got to make sure you can explain to them what the alternative punishments will be. And listen, if other students see that some of the kids are getting out of having to serve detention and they start to argue and ask you about it, just say, "Ohhhh, is that so? You think he is getting out of detention? Well, first of all, you have no idea how bad his punishment is. Second, don't be so sure he is missing detention. And third of all, it is none of your business." The kid who is being punished might not serve the detention, but you can't let on that is the case. I mean, the kid might tell everyone he doesn't have to go and he is getting an alternate punishment, but you just keep on playing the game as if that boy just doesn't know what's in store for him. I know it seems strange, but it works. Just *never* tell the class that you are substituting punishments for certain people.

Four Checks

Usually after I give out a detention slip, the student will try very hard to behave, and rarely will anyone get four checks. I tell the students that with four checks, there will be an immediate parent-teacher conference about the behavior. When it does happen, depending on the severity of the action, different forms of parent contact will occur. For example, if I don't feel it is a serious problem, I will just wait and call the parent when I get home. If it is more of a problem, I will call during planning time or after school. On some occasions, I will ask the child to step out in the hall, and I will call the parent on my cell phone. I don't do that often, because it interrupts the class. I will, however, do it every now and then, because I want the students to know that if I need to, I can have their parents on the phone at a moment's notice. There have been times when a student's behavior has warranted a parent-teacher conference with the principal present. When this happens, I always make sure to have documentation of the student's behavior. For example, I have a list of each day the child has had silent lunch, copies of signed detention slips, and a written explanation of the actions that led up to the four checks.

These consequences may seem harsh, and honestly, for the first few weeks of school I always have half of the class sitting with me at silent lunch, missing recess, and spending days in detention. After about a month, though, everyone begins to understand what they need to do to avoid getting in trouble, and there are far fewer punishments to hand out. There is a lot of work for the teacher in the beginning, but in the end, it all pays off.

The consequences are necessary; they are the key to getting kids to perform. Each year, before going over the rules, I give a speech to the students. The message in the speech is one that I deliver several times throughout the year. I believe it when I say it to the students, so I say it with passion and they know I mean it. It goes something like this:

> This year has the possibility of being one of the best years of your life. If you are willing to listen to me and do as I ask, we can make amazing things happen. You

have got to believe me, and you have got to trust me. I am going to give 110 percent and work my hardest to make sure you get the best education possible. I don't care what kind of grades you have had in the past, and I don't care what kind of trouble you have been in before; this is a new year, and we are going to have a new start, and I assure you, if you are willing to follow the rules and procedures and try your best, this year you will all be stars. Not only can we be the best class in this school, we can be the best class in this country.

It may seem hokey, but the thing is, I honestly believe it is possible, and therefore, it *is* possible. I would believe it no matter which thirty kids in the country you placed in my classroom.

It is important that I deliver my message in a certain way; as I say those words I am animated, moving from side to side, looking the students in their eyes, and speaking with conviction. As I look around the room, I can see in their faces that they are starting to believe it. Why? Well, because quite simply they want to believe it is possible; they want to believe it is true.

A final component to getting children to perform deals with giving rewards. When students do well, you need to let them know it. One of the main rewards I use is good old-fashioned praise. In all opportunities possible I let kids know the things they have done well and the talents they have in certain areas. I have found it is effective to praise a child one-on-one, but I have seen the biggest influence on students when I give them accolades in front of others. When used in front of other students, praise can be a very powerful persuasion technique.

When I was teaching in North Carolina, there was a child named Arlis who really did poorly at most subjects. He was a solid D student, and quite often he failed the majority of his courses. In North Carolina you have to take end-of-grade tests in fifth grade in math and reading, and in order to be on grade level you must score a level 3, meaning you are on grade level, or level 4, meaning you are above grade level. Levels 1 and 2 designate students who are below grade level, and those in level 1 are required to attend summer school or repeat the grade. The year before, Arlis had scored low level 2's, and even though I saw a great deal of potential in him, he was very disinterested in school, and I was afraid he would fall in the level 1 category in fifth grade.

In the first month of the school year, we were reading *The Lion, the Witch, and the Wardrobe,* and I asked the class to predict what was going to happen in the next chapter, which was titled "Deeper Magic from the Dawn of Time." Arlis raised his hand and said, "I think there is going to be an older spell that is good that is going to cancel out the bad one." He couldn't have been more correct, and let me tell you, I sure milked that for all it was worth. I pointed out to all the kids how brilliant his prediction was and how proud of him I was for figuring that out. Then I asked a few of my colleagues to do me a favor and mention to Arlis that they had heard he made some really good observations about the novel we were reading. I called his mom and told her I was proud of Arlis for paying attention during reading and that he was doing an excellent job of participating in class. Was I going a little overboard? Well, maybe so, but it sure began to pay off.

When we would get to a new chapter and I would ask for predictions, Arlis's hand was the first to be in the air. He wasn't always right, but I would act as if I hadn't really noticed that. For example, no matter how "out there" his answers were, instead of saying he was wrong, I would say something like, "Oh, I can see where you're coming from, Arlis, but can someone tell me . . ." I was working very hard to build up his confidence, and the last thing I wanted to do was tear it down. Sometimes while we were reading I would say something to this effect, "That was a really difficult passage, and I want to make sure you all understand what the author was really trying to say. I mean, I'm sure Arlis and a few others of you understood it, but I want to make sure we all get the big picture."

By the end of the year, Arlis had become one of my best reading students, and he scored a level 4 on his end-of-grade reading test. Simply through receiving that praise and building his confidence, he began to believe he was an exceptional reader, and in the process, he became one. Of course, high expectations, individual instruction, and other motivating factors all played into Arlis's success, but I know that the key, without a doubt, was praise.

Sometimes, however, praise is not enough. I usually take my students on twenty-five to thirty small trips a year, but I don't necessarily take the entire class each time. I usually begin the year by taking small trips with just three or four kids. That is a very manageable number, and we usually go somewhere that doesn't require a lot of planning or extra effort on my part, like the movies or a museum. It's quick and it's easy, but it will have a definite impact on the climate of the class. When the other students find out I took a group to the movies, they wonder why they weren't picked. They want to know what they have to do to get picked. I usually select the initial group for behaving well or doing good work, so it translates into good motivation for the rest of the class.

I eventually take larger trips with the kids where the entire class is invited, but anyone who is not performing as he or she is supposed to be will not be invited to go. The trips can be really fun as well, like trips to professional basketball games, the beach, amusement parks, and all different types of cultural events. Each year there is also at least one overnight trip that can work as major motivation. One thing I have learned, though, about a major trip is that you never want to use that as a form of punishment. Not getting to go on such a fun and exciting and educational trip can really scar a kid. I have had to battle that one out with parents numerous times. They don't feel their child deserves to go because of poor grades or behavior, but I tell them that not allowing the child to go can end up doing a lot more harm than good.

Once I arranged to take a group of twelve students to attend a practice of the North Carolina Tar Heels basketball team. For those kids, it was like a dream, and they were all thrilled about going. In order to prepare, they had to use the players' statistics in order to complete math worksheets and other assignments. They also had to study the history of the university and the basketball program. A few days before we were to go, one of the students, Rodriquez, hadn't learned all of the information and hadn't turned in his worksheets. I told him, in front of the other students, that if he didn't have them the next day he wouldn't be allowed to go. The next day he frantically walked in and claimed he couldn't finish the worksheets because he had left one of them at school. I told him, without blinking an eye, that he couldn't go. I could tell he was destroyed, but it was obvious he was trying to hide that from the other students. The entire time we were at the Dean Dome, I kept thinking about Rodriquez and how much that experience would have meant to him. The students were even allowed to shoot around with some of the Tar Heel players. It was a once-in-a-lifetime opportunity, and I had denied Rodriquez the chance to go. No, he didn't complete his work, but I never should have said he wouldn't be allowed to go if he didn't turn in those worksheets. In some cases, stipulations like that shouldn't be used. You just have to look at the big picture and ask yourself what, in the end, is best for the child. A better punishment for Rodriquez would have been to have him stay after school every day for a week doing extra work. I should have never put his chances of going on the trip in jeopardy. Taking away some things is okay, and of course it's okay to punish kids by denying them privileges, but we should never deny them experiences that could motivate and inspire them or change their lives for the better.

I have one more comment about rewards and punishments—they should be given immediately after the action. Dealing with administration can sometimes make that impossible. In some schools, if a child is written up for a disciplinary action, it could be days before the child is called to the office or disciplined in any way. Sometimes schools will name a "Student of the Week." That child is supposed to receive some reward like free ice cream from the principal, but it could be weeks before it actually happens. Imagine how we would feel if our paycheck (our reward) were two weeks late. Have mercy, I know I would be living on cucumber sandwiches and crackers. What if during a basketball game a referee blew his whistle for a foul that was committed in the last quarter? It just doesn't make sense.

I remember one time I put the students on teams of seven and told them that I would order a pizza for the group that scored the highest on their Friday spelling test. Well, that week I saw the highest spelling scores of the year, and the winning group ended up scoring all 100's. They were thrilled and were all ready for the pizza that day, but I forgot to call in time for the pizza to get there for lunch. I told them I would order it on the following Monday, but then two of the kids from the team were absent. Before I knew it, it was Friday again, and they still hadn't gotten their pizza. Needless to say, that Friday I saw some of the lowest test scores of the year.

On the other hand, I had two students get in a fight in the bathroom one morning. Why must they always start the fights in the bathroom? There I go, running in, slipping and sliding, grabbing one boy with one hand and one in the other. They were huffing and puffing and furious, and I took them down to the office to see the principal. She said she would deal with them immediately, but as our class walked by on the way to the lunchroom, I noticed the boys still sitting in the office. They said they had not even seen the principal yet, so I just took them with us to eat. After lunch, I talked with both boys, and we worked out the problem. That happened on a Wednesday. The following Monday, the in-school-suspension teacher arrived and said the boys were to spend two days with her for punishment. At that time, the boys were fine, they were doing their work, and they were focused on what was going on in class. The incidents surrounding the fight were far removed from their minds, yet they were now, almost a week later, being punished. It reminds me of a story my sister told me recently. She said Austin, my nephew, was acting up in Kmart, but she had to wait two hours until she got home before she could put him in time-out. She said he didn't even remember why he was being punished.

In order to be effective, discipline and praise must be given immediately. The closer they are given to the occurrence, the more influence they will have on the child.

IN CLOSING . . .

When I finished writing this book, I was one happy person. Getting so many thoughts, ideas, and stories on paper was much harder than I first anticipated, and I thought I was finally done when my best friend, Amanda, asked me, "So, how does your book end? I just *hate* it when a book doesn't have a good ending." I took a deep breath and gulped. I respect her opinion, and her statement scared the death out of me. How am I supposed to end this book? Well, for starters, I know at least Amanda is going to like this ending because her name is in it (Amanda Rae Nixon from Hope Mills, North Carolina), but for everyone else I felt like it needed something more. Then, as I tried to decide on an ending, I was talking with my co-teacher from Snowden Elementary School, Barbara Jones, and she said to me, "So, Mr. Clark, please tell me you wrote in the book what your meaning of life is. I love to hear you talk about it." I hadn't mentioned it up to that point, and it seemed like a fitting ending, so here goes . . .

To me, life is all about experiences, the ones you make for yourself and the ones you make for others. As a teacher, and as a person, I have tried to give special moments to people. I mentioned earlier that I once took students to the campus of the University of North Carolina to watch a col'ege basketball practice. When it was over, I got to tell the 'udents, "Kids, I know I told you we were only here to \tch, but you all need to go get changed, because we're ng to get to play a game in the Dean Dome!" I can still ember the look on Kenny Brown's face as he jumped up lown over and over. The expression in his eyes was by, total elation, and shock. I know that is a moment never forget as long as he lives.

Moments like that occurred when I announced to the students they were going to the White House, surprised the students in Harlem with the trip to Los Angeles, had my students in the front rows of *Phantom of the Opera,* and every time I put my students in situations where they felt totally alive and knew that they were truly living. Giving them those types of moments, making those types of emotions for others, is, to me, what life is about. If this book has done nothing else, I hope it has inspired you to make more of a difference in the lives of children. Guide them as they grow, show them in every way possible that they are cared for, and make special moments for them that will add magic to their lives, motivate them to make a difference in the lives of others, and, most important, teach them to love life.